Remembering
REPUTATION
and PROSPERITY

A Story of the American West

A.G. Roeber

ELEVATION PRESS
OF COLORADO

Remembering Reputation and Prosperity: A Story of the American West

By A.G. Roeber

Copyright © 2024 by A.G. Roeber

For more information, please see *About the Author* at the close of this book.

Cover design and interior design and formatting by Donna Marie Benjamin.

Photo credits:
Photo 1981129 | Wood Background | Piro4D | Pixabay.com
Photo 19337801 | Border © Almir1968 | Dreamstime.com
Photo 29409141 | Parchment © James Larkin | Dreamstime.com
Back cover photo courtesy of Mt. Lamborn Ranches

All rights reserved. No part of this publication may be reproduced, distributed, or transmitted in any form or by any means, including photocopying, recording, or other electronic or mechanical methods, without the prior written permission of the publisher, except in the case of brief quotations embodied in critical reviews and certain other noncommercial uses permitted by copyright law. For permission requests, write to the author at the address below:

Agr2@psu.edu

Ordering information: Quantity sales. Special discounts are available on quantity purchases by book clubs, corporations, associations, and others. For details, contact the publisher at the address above.

ISBN 978-0-932624-28-4

1. Main category—[History] 2. Other categories—[Immigration]—[Philosophy/Memory]— [Family/ Genealogy]—[American West]

Cedaredge, Colorado
www.elevation-press-books.com

A New Family History

A.G. Roeber's new family history traces his ancestors from poor butcher shops in 16th century Saxony to the "German Mesa" on the western slope of the Colorado Rockies. No simple heroic pioneer tale, theirs is a tangled story of risk and ambition, marriage and divorce, births and untimely deaths, of striving for success, seizing opportunities, settling down, uprooting and settling again, always adapting to forces beyond their control. The intersections of private lives with public narratives make this account unusually insightful. Employing every trick of a professional historian, Roeber extracts "facts" from all sorts of documentary records, then sifts the fragments, blending them with (often contradictory) first-person recollections, to construct a surprisingly rich account of an "ordinary" family. This book rewards readers in two different ways. Friends and family of the Roeber clan will find details about genealogy, land transactions, and the occasional "character" in the ancestral attic. Others may read this book as a micro-history showing how much we can and cannot recover about the lives, habits, and possessions of people who did not expect to become the subjects of a historian's inquiry.

—John L. Larson, Professor of History, Purdue University. Author of *Laid Waste! The Culture of Exploitation in Early America* (Penn Press, 2019).

Roeber Family Tree

Georg Röber, senior (1587–1658) married Catherina (surname unknown)

Georg Röber, junior (1619–1690) married Maria, (surname unknown) 1651

Christian Röber (1659–1723) married Anna Regine Fleischer 1685

George Röber (1689–1748) married Anna Sophia Knödel 1714/ she died 1723; second marriage to Maria Christina Strehle 1724

Carl Gottlob Röber, senior (1736–1811) married Rosina Maria Klotz 1758

Carl Gottlob Röber, junior (1759–1821) married Johanna Rebecca Felber 1783

Karl August Röber (1784–1823) married Johanna Beata Glöckner 1809

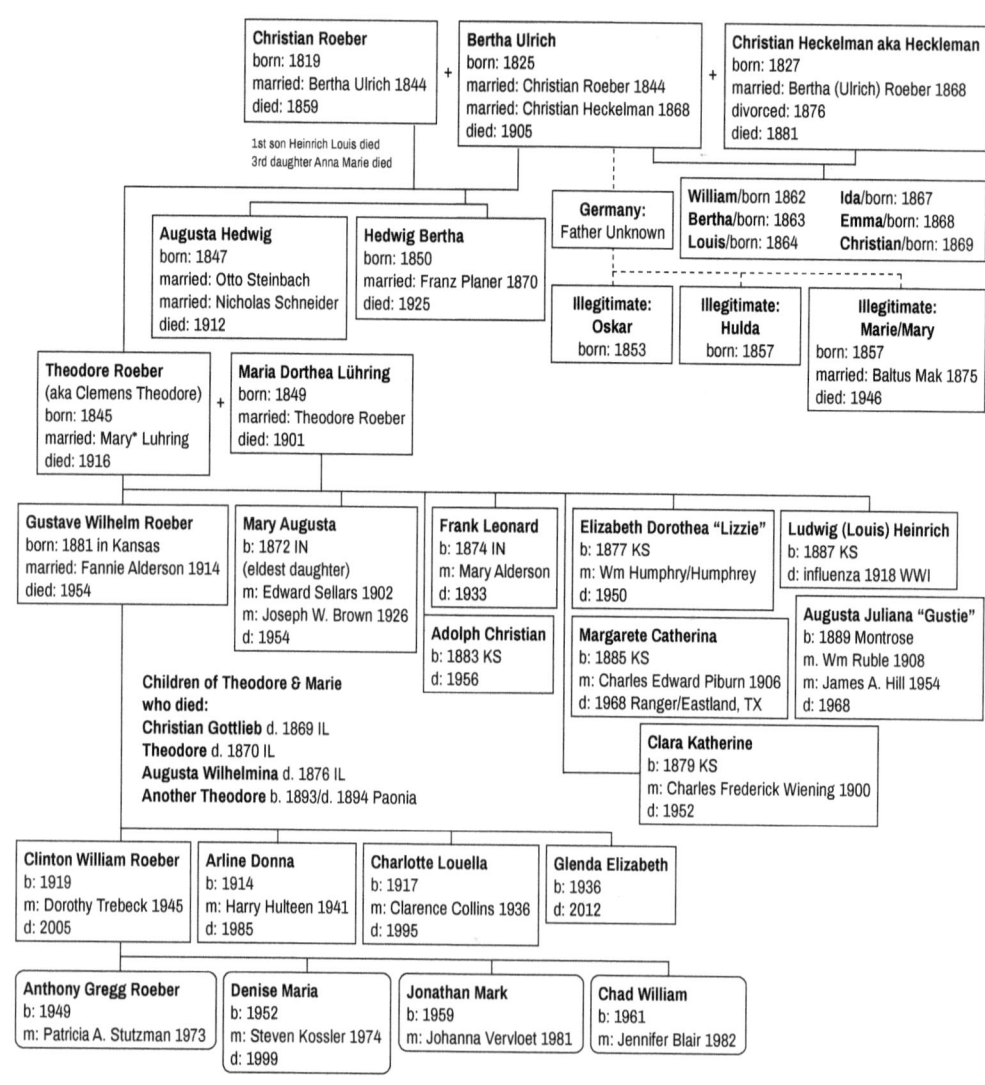

Introduction

Readers familiar with the history of the Trans-Mississippi American West range from professional, academic historians to interested descendants of the First Peoples of North America and all subsequent arrivals and visitors. Some parts of the American West have received detailed attention, the degree of research and writing dictated by what has survived and that survival itself has been dependent largely upon whether a degree of prosperity has encouraged preservation of personal and public records. Professional historians also know about and struggle to engage the problem of memory—often in the form of oral and written accounts, both individual and collective. Such memories have proven to provide especially challenging questions of assessment and interpretation of evidence.

This book is no exception. It is not intended as an academic, professional volume. Its "target audience" will hopefully be a much broader set of readers and to that end, I have relegated to the end of each chapter a list of sources used for those who wish to pursue in more scholarly detail what the narrative has relied on but tries to put succinctly. The original documents have been donated to the Roeber Family Collection in the Archives and Special Collections of the Tomlinson Library at Colorado Mesa University in Grand Junction. This book uses the history of one family name in both documented and memory forms as a lens into a relatively neglected county of Colorado's Western Slope from the 1880s to the present. In doing so, it explores what Colorado historians have long emphasized—that what became the *Centennial*

State in 1876 has routinely experienced cycles of *boom and bust*. The efforts of individuals to secure a modest degree of economic security, social standing, and acceptance of competing ways of life and ancestral origins could be claimed to be the larger story of the United States as a whole.

What this book also attempts, however, is to cast a glance back wherever possible at the places of origin outside of the United States and the fate of those who did not emigrate. That move helps to shed additional light and explanation for the choices made by those who settled in western Colorado and who continue to do so and how local choices have always been linked to broader national and international issues even when those connections have not been clear to the participants.

The area today known as Delta County, Colorado has attracted the attention of earlier writers, beginning in the 1930s with Wilson Rockwell's *New Frontier*. But the only academic, professional history of the Western Slope remains the 1981 book by Duane Vandenbusche and Duane A. Smith, *A Land Alone: Colorado's Western Slope,* and understandably, the North Fork of the Gunnison River Valley only occasionally appears in their assessments. As any reader familiar with that book will quickly see, I share many of their judgments and conclusions, perhaps evident in the title I've chosen to give the book.

I began my own academic study of Colorado history at the University of Denver in 1971 and profited from the insights gained by my then-professors Carl Abbott who in 1976 published the first edition of his *Colorado: A History of the Centennial State* and the late Michael McGiffert who had already in 1964 authored *The Higher Education in Colorado: An Historical Study, 1860–1940*. Although I completed an independent study at DU on the career of the Montrose-based lawyer and Populist Party congressman John C. Bell, the thesis I finally wrote focused on the connections between religious and political identities during the turbulent 1890s in the city of Denver. I have had little reason to retract or revise the conclusions I came to then, but interested parties can consult the copy of that thesis: "The Politics of Religious Identity: Roman Catholicism in Colorado, 1892–1896," M.A. thesis,

Department of History, University of Denver, 1972. My copy of the thesis is now part of the Mesa University Special Collections.

Collections of stories and memories of the North Fork of the Gunnison area have appeared in the books authored by Laura Clock, Mamie Ferrier, Muriel Marshall, Glen Haley, and my own father, Clinton Roeber. In the 1960s, a collection of stories produced in typescript by my father's oldest sister Arline (Roeber) Hulteen and her cousin Dorothy Sellars attempted to reconstruct the remote history and arrival of Clemens Theodore Roeber and his wife Maria Dorothea Lühring to the Western Slope and their settlement on what was then known as "German Mesa" in Delta County in 1889. A copy of that effort has also been deposited with the other sources available at Mesa University.

I will add two brief notes regarding my use of names and quotations. Depending upon the source, Theodore Roeber's wife was called either "Maria" or "Mary." Because she later gave birth to a daughter also named Maria, I have chosen to avoid confusion by referring to the wife as Maria and her eldest natural daughter as Mary. As for quotations from original source documents, these contain occasional misspellings which are generally understood in context. Where such misspellings may puzzle the reader, I have added an explanatory "translation."

The happy discovery of Theodore Roeber's copy of his original baptismal certificate issued in Gersdorf, Kingdom of Saxony in 1845 opened the door to a more accurate, documented history that required substantial revision of the memories collected by his granddaughters. At times, readers who are not related to the family will encounter genealogical information that can be skipped or skimmed quickly, but which is of some real significance for family members.

CHAPTER ONE

Remembering a Name

Sometime during the early 1950s, as I was walking down the main street of the town of Paonia, Colorado where I had been born, an elderly man stopped me and said, "You're Gus Rayber's grandson, aren't you?" Momentarily perplexed about the pronunciation of my last name, I still managed to say, "Yes, I am." It was not until decades later that I came to understand that this contemporary of my grandfather, Gustave Wilhelm Röber, was using the pronunciation my grandfather himself would have used, as generations of our ancestors before him would have done.

In exploring my family's roots, I have come to three conclusions: 1) the name Roeber has existed in a variety of spellings; 2) the Old World ancestral Roeber family lived and worked in a variety of eastern German regions but primarily in communities known today as Görlitz and Zschopau; and 3) those ancestors were primarily members of the butcher trade. The remainder of this chapter summarizes evidence which supports these conclusions.

The common Saxon pronunciation of the German "o" vowel with the "umlaut" sometimes realized as an "e" even today results in the "ay" sound for the name "Roeber." Less clear is what the family name means. Many possibilities exist, but no memory of the word's meaning survived among those members of what had once been a very large family who eventually emigrated to North America in the mid-nineteenth century.

The famous nineteenth-century German language dictionary compiled by the brothers Grimm *(Grimmisches Wörterbuch)* found variations of the family name all over German-speaking Europe. There exist such wildly divergent spellings as to make a place of origin or even the meaning of the term nearly impossible to determine. Those variations include: Roever, Röver, Röbe, Rübe, Ruderer, Rauber, Räuber. In the more hilly or mountainous regions (hence, "High" Germany) in modern-day Thuringia a place called "Roben" can be found and some have speculated that perhaps the word meant those from that particular settlement.

Two surviving coats of arms also reveal different places and different status of the men granted those honors. One appears in 1537. That coat of arms given to three individuals (who were not nobility): Martin Schmidt, Hans Miller and Georg Reuber identifies them as men who had conducted themselves as "wise and deliberate orators in the Moskowiterei legation under King Maximilian I." The reference to the Holy Roman Emperor Maximilian (1493–1519) indicates service done during his reign. However, the granting of this particular coat of arms was given at Prague on 24 April 1537 by "King Ferdinand" (1503–64) who was already King of Bohemia, Hungary and Croatia from 1526 and would later become Holy Roman Emperor.

Since the coat of arms includes a "springing white hare" with a "Tartar Man" swinging a saber, it may be the case that the three aforementioned men were involved in negotiations between the Holy Roman Empire and the Ottoman Empire or with Russian Tartary, the Crimean Tartary or another Central Asian leader. The award could also have resulted from negotiations between the Emperor Maximilian and the King of Hungary Matthias Corvinus (1443–1519). That monarch claimed sovereignty over the area along the Neiße River, today part of southeastern Germany but, in medieval times, more commonly known as "Lusatia" or the Lausitz. Even place names have proven elusive. The name *Lausitz* does not appear prior to the 1370s when it referred to Budissin, in the "lower," i.e. in the *flat lands* along the Neiße River but gradually extended to include the "upper" lands of rolling hills and the river town of Görlitz.

In this region, an economic union of six towns from 1346 received the royal approval of the King of Bohemia. These half-dozen towns enjoyed a close tie to that royal house while landed nobles in the surrounding countryside—who had a reputation for being dangerous brigands and were forbidden to build castles by the Bohemian King—still controlled much of the political destiny of the region. Political claims on this territory shifted from those made by the ruler of Bohemia (today the Czech Republic), by the King of Hungary, and much later by the Saxon rulers who were Electors within the Holy Roman Empire. Electors were those casting a vote for who would be Holy Roman Emperor. Of the major six towns that were part of the 1346 union, Görlitz played a central role in the history of at least that branch of the family that eventually came to be known as "Roeber."

It is in this town that one also encounters yet another reason for the different spellings of this family name. Along the Neiße River, German-speaking as well as Slavic (Sorb)-speaking settlers had established settlements since around the year 1000. The "Upper Lusatian" area—meaning the territory in the foothills toward the modern border with the Czech Republic—developed a language affinity with Czech, and inhabitants continued to speak Sorbian or Wendish, the Slavic language of the area. By the fifteenth century, the eastern part of Upper Lusatia, including the town of Görlitz, was predominantly German-speaking and in the year 1586 this prosperous town boasted some 8,685 inhabitants. Already by the 1400s, German became increasingly the favored official language as the territory more closely integrated with the politics of Saxony and the Holy Roman Empire, even though Saxony did not rule Lusatia. Place names such as Görlitz reflect the Slavic origin (here meaning "burned land," i.e. subject to de-forestation) and the region's mix of German- and Sorb-speakers possibly points to the Roeber family name as originally Sorbic. In its later Germanized form, it remains even today a relatively rare name in Germany or Austria. References survive to a Georg Räuber (1587–1658) and another man (1619–1690) of the same name and finally, to a member of the Görlitz shooting club, Sigmund who was lauded as the best shot at a match in 1601, the oldest member of the guild who died a year later in 1602.

We cannot know for certain what occupations these men and their spouses and children followed to make a living. But research carried out by Pastor Klaus Roeber of Berlin in the archives of the church and town in Görlitz found evidence of dwellings belonging to this family along the riverbank and he also discovered the suggestion that they made their living by fishing. If we consider the spelling of key terms in Wendish, we can see that the family was not known as "robbers" for that word in Wendish is *rubjeznik*. The word for "fish" on the other hand, is *ryba* and "fishing" *rybarstwo*. Those words are closer to the "Reuber" or "Räuber," the earliest Germanized form of the name. But far to the northeast in what became part of the territory of Brandenburg-Prussia, another coat of arms survives, and it points to a line called "Röber von Röbern" which had become extinct by the time the volumes of both noble and middling coats of arms were compiled.

Other tantalizing hints survive in the persons of two individuals. The Lutheran theologian and pastor Paulus Röber (1587–1651) was born in the town of Wurzen, a few kilometers northeast of Leipzig. However, nothing in his career or his known associates ties him to possible kinsmen farther to the south on the borders between Saxony and Bohemia. On that border, and somewhat closer to the Ore Mountains in a location that would be the origin of the Roeber family members who emigrated to North America, and closer in time to that emigration, Friedrich August Röber (1765–1827) achieved a modicum of fame as the city physician in the Saxon capital Dresden. By the early nineteenth century, a group of Lutheran dissidents led by a charismatic pastor Martin Stefan were suspected of disturbing the peace of the Saxon Kingdom. Stefan was examined by the city physician who gave as his professional opinion the likelihood that Stefan was mentally unbalanced. Perhaps not surprisingly, the later relationship of the Roeber family in America to these dissidents—who eventually became known in North America as "The German Evangelical Lutheran Church of Missouri and Other States" was never especially close.

Unfortunately, the destruction of parish church records during the Thirty Years' War (1618–1648) in the town of Zschopau, which lies further to the western areas of Saxony where the American branch of this family can be traced accurately, has made it impossible to establish a firm link between the Görlitz family of fishermen, the Lutheran pastor, or the Dresden physician and our ancestral family of butchers and meat purveyors from Zschopau. A close connection between that town and Görlitz surfaces in the person of a daughter of the Görlitz Röber family, Anna, who married the mayor of the large town of Chemnitz which lies only a few miles to the northwest of Zschopau. In that latter town, a documented history of the "Roeber" family can be reconstructed in some detail—a history in which mysteries, and perhaps forgotten memories, shed some light on the constant threat of poverty and social dislocation, as well as the allure of better conditions and times elsewhere.

In order to appreciate the significance of occupations, marriage patterns, and political and religious connections of this family group, we need to bear in mind the origins of the town of Zschopau near the larger town of Chemnitz (whose own original Slavic name was from *kamenica* or *kamjen* meaning "stone"). The possibility of a link between the two towns and the family names comes from the fact that the earliest surviving church records in Zschopau refer to a Georg Reuber (1587–1658). The spelling of the name changed over the course of the seventeenth and eighteenth centuries to Räuber (a version the family probably did not appreciate given its sounding like the German "robber") and by the 1700s consistently to Röber.

The foregoing spelling changes might suggest a "Germanization" of the family name as well as their town of residence, since Zschopau is Slavic in origin. In the oldest surviving records (from the year 981) the place appears as *Tzschachpe, Scopa, Scapa, Zopa, Tschopa, Tskchope, Tzchopa, Tzschoppe, Szpopwa*—variations meaning "the place of passage." The town was built on a small river of that same name in the early 1200s. By 1292, it was designated as a "Stadt" or city which was located on the medieval trade road that connected the larger cities of Chemnitz in Saxony, a few kilometers to the northwest, while passing through the Ore Mountains *(Erzgebirge)* to Prague, the seat of power of the rulers of Bohemia.

The Zschopau River arises from springs at the Fichtelberg, the highest mountain in Saxony, flows north through the towns of Schlettau and

Wolkenstein, past Zschopau, then further northward to Flöhe, and finally into the larger river, the Freiberger Mulda. A small tower named the *Wildeck* arose in 1299 on the riverbank and provided the ruling authorities with a lookout toward the south, in the direction of the rising, deeply forested hill country. The tower eventually served as a hunting lodge. In 1307 the small city received its first Catholic priest and between 1349 and 1407 the discovery of silver ore transformed the landscape and gave the nearby mountain range its name. Not only did mines now spring up in the hills around the river valley, but many of the hills were deforested to provide both charcoal for smelting furnaces and transport vehicles for the silver ore. By 1451 the city received the privilege of holding an open market. The prosperity of these years led to the construction of a second church in 1454, a funerary chapel dedicated to the Virgin Mary on the other side of the river beyond the city walls. After receiving the privilege of being identified as a *Bergstadt*—a town associated with the mining of precious minerals—in 1493, a subsequent increase in population led to the building of a new and expanded church, town hall, and city walls.

This wave of prosperity, however, lasted only until about 1560, part of a long history of *boom and bust* which over the centuries has produced vast wealth for a small percentage of the population, but left the majority in times of dire poverty and near-starvation, with social and political consequences that began to be clear already in the 16th century. By the mid-1500s, the entire region began to feel the impact of the importation of vast quantities of silver from the Spanish exploration and exploitation of the Americas. Although both silver and tin mining continued in this middle-Ore Mountain region, Zschopau did not become the center of the more elaborate religious and secular structures that arose, for example, further to the south in Annaberg. Nor did the town participate in a major way in the most disruptive and controversial social and political uprising in sixteenth-century Central Europe—the Peasant Rebellion of 1525.

The supporters of the uprising were miners but came from the mining towns of Annaberg-Buchholz, Marienberg, and smaller locations. In response to demands made by the alarmed Elector Georg of Saxony, the town fathers in Zschopau hastened to assure him of their obedience and loyalty. The use of the first name "Georg" by two generations of male members of this Zschopau family apparently reflected some degree of deference or honor paid to the current ruler. The House of Wettin had, since medieval times, dominated the history of what would later become central and eastern Germany. That dominant house divided its territories in 1485 at the Treaty of Leipzig. Originally, the older line of the family known as the "Ernestine" held the electoral dignity and included territories that became known as Saxe-Coburg and Saxe-Gotha, all of which supported the Reformation. The younger branch of the family, the "Albertine," was centered on the city of Dresden. This branch was known as "ducal Saxony" but because it supported the Holy Roman Emperor Charles V in the Schmalkaldic War between Catholic and Lutheran partisans, it was rewarded with the electoral dignity.

As a result of these alliances, the Röbers began then, in Görlitz as subjects of Lusatia and eventually the Albertine Wettins. But after the first generation in Zschopau, male descendants in the Röber family seldom chose to name their sons after the current reigning Elector, and later, King. The Electors Christian (I and II) reigned from 1586 to 1611, followed by a series of Johann Georgs from 1611 to 1694. The name Augustus had appeared among the electors from 1553 to 1586 and then again as Frederick Augustus from 1763 to 1827 and the King Frederick Augustus II from 1836 to 1854. But the first names of the successive generations of the Röbers of Zschopau and later Gersdorf do not appear to have been chosen out of any reverence or deference to the House of Wettin.

By the 1600s, both lines of the House of Wettin had adopted agnatic primogeniture laws which applied not only to the nobility but also to propertied commoners. Those laws held that the eldest male inherited the entire property with the obligation to provide some compensation to his younger siblings and to protect the rights of a surviving widow. This practice was formally adopted in 1831 when Saxony became a parliamentary monarchy. Some provisions were made for a female successor in the absence of a male heir in the ruling house. Voting rights were tied to ownership of property. The right to emigrate was guaranteed as long as the male heir was not facing civil obligations or military service. These provisions explain in part why, in the history of the large Röber family in Zschopau, even some younger sons from the sixteenth to the early nineteenth century were employed as butchers even if they were not the eldest son and heir. By the early nineteenth century, however, circumstances would arise that forced a younger son not only out of the traditional family occupation, but out of Zschopau itself.

Toward the end of the sixteenth century, Zschopau became the center of religious controversy that erupted after the posthumous discovery of the writings of its most famous Lutheran pastor, Valentin Weigel, who served his parish faithfully from 1567 to 1588. One year before his death, Weigel baptized Georg Räuber, Senior (1587–1658) whose house still was in ruins in 1657 following the burning of the town by imperial troops during the Thirty Years' War (1618–1648). Weigel's mysticism and beliefs in an inner spiritual life that was not dependent on sacred scripture brought his writings (discovered only after his death) into disrepute and condemnation by Lutheran theologians. His successor in Zschopau, Pastor Benedikt Biedermann, lost his pastorate in the town in 1599 when an investigation of his library revealed his ownership of Weigel's manuscript writings. Because of the later destruction of baptismal records, we can only guess at the exact identity of Elias Röber, born in 1597, possibly a younger brother of Georg, almost certainly baptized by Pastor Biedermann, but known only from the date of his death in 1659. What we do know is that the surviving church records consistently identify the members of this family as butchers *(Fleischhauer)*. Both Elias and Georg Sr. survived the outbreak of plague that ravished the town in 1612 killing some 476 persons. Eight years later, Georg Röber the younger was born and, by the time he stood as godfather for an acquaintance, he was also identified as a butcher. (Georg stood as godfather to Maria, the daughter of Georg and Rosina Achhäusser—Maria's husband was identified as a handworker dyer of black fabric or *Schwarzfärber*).

Both men and women, if they entertained the decision to marry, were constrained by the laws of the established church, the Evangelical (Lutheran) Church of Electoral Saxony. Prohibitions on marrying those of close blood relatives had not changed significantly because of the Reformation. In order to avoid the possibility of marrying someone who might be a cousin, spouses were regularly sought out from neighboring villages and towns. The surviving church records in Zschopau reveal this pattern for the Roeber family. Spouses came from as far away as Ottendorf, northwest of Chemnitz, or the larger town of Döbeln near the confluence of the Zschopau River and the larger Freiberger Mulda. But most lived in villages a few kilometers away in Kunnersdorf, Erdmannsdorf, Waldkirchen, Gornau, Hausdorf, Hennersdorf, that is, from the Zschopau river valley and predominantly from the north, not from the mining areas in the south of this valley. Family occupations of the future wives' fathers ranged from butchers, millers, linen weavers, bakers, hatmakers, carpenters, clothiers, to the chief town official and local judge (*Erbrichter*) and a tax assessor temporarily living in the town.

Working primarily as butchers, the Roeber family may have occupied a unique area of Zschopau. Surviving records locate the town's original house, the slaughterhouse, at the end of the *Bergstraße* (the street leading toward the hills) with unused or decaying animal parts dumped into the ravine outside the town walls. The meat stall erected on the central marketplace provided the space where the modestly prosperous members of this family lived and worked. Ultimately, that stability and membership in the *Kleinbürgertum,* or petty bourgeoisie, fell victim, as did the entire town, to the catastrophe of the Thirty Years' War.

In 1632, some 14 years after the outbreak of the conflict, Croatian troops in the pay of the Holy Roman Emperor sacked the town, causing those who could do so to flee into the forests near Grünhainichen where they hid themselves in the rocky cliffs. By 1634, the town had been burned and what remained was expropriated and Swedish imperial troops quartered on the site. A year before the Treaty of Westphalia brought the war in central Europe to an end, the parish church of St. Martin that had been destroyed with the rest of the town was re-built, re-dedicated and blessed in 1649. The cornerstone for a church tower was not laid until 1688 and only finished in 1697; the interior of the church was restored to include an organ built by the Leipzig organ builder Christoph Donat the Elder. However, the most striking surviving interior iconography of the earlier church is the 1609 portrayal of the Parable of the Good Samaritan. In picturing the scene of a priest hurrying past the man who had fallen among robbers, the unknown artist chose to portray the Jewish priest as a Catholic priest. The Levite, who also ignores the victim, appears in the guise of a Lutheran clergyman. And the Good Samaritan is unmistakably a Turkish Muslim.

How the town butcher's family survived the harrowing events of the mid-seventeenth century remains unknown and was never committed to written or oral memory. The church records of marriages and burials (from 1648) suggest that Georg Röber Sr. was widowed but married again in 1631. Between 1632 and 1643, another seven children were born to this second marriage, and among them, Michael's baptism revealed one result of the chaos of the Thirty Years' War. This child was baptized by the midwife *(Wehemutter)* because the pastor and his family had already fled to escape the capture by Croatian imperial troops—a fate that befell the parish deacon.

The ruined condition of the town was still obvious when Georg Röber Jr. married his wife Maria in 1651. Only 17 years old at the time, she was not from Zschopau nor did the marriage take place in her husband's parish church. Only three years after this marriage, fire broke out in the brewery of the town and consumed the house of Georg Röber Sr. who must have begun rebuilding sometime after the end of the war in 1648. This time, the ruins remained as late as 1657 when the church records noted that "…an old soldier died on the ruins of Georg Röber the Elder's house at whose entrance he was looking for bread…"

Nonetheless, when Georg Sr. died a year later at the age of 71, he was identified as butcher and citizen of the town and buried from the church with a funeral service accompanied by choral music. A year later, his son Georg Jr. and daughter-in-law Maria had a fourth child, Christian (1659–1723).

(This particular Christian may have been the member of this family to have had at least a brief brush with royalty. In 1699, when Christian would have been 40 years old, Tsar Peter the Great of Russia halted in the town at the White Horse Inn when one of his carriage wheels broke. Entertained at the tower now called the *Castle Wildeck*, the Tsar asked to be shown the technical workings of the looms operated by the local stocking weavers. The record of the visit does not, alas, give a first name to a "certain Röber" who conducted the tour. At the time of the Tsar's visit Zschopau contained 378 houses and an adult population of 1,124. On the town marketplace the butcher's stall, a one-story building, boasted nine windows and a tiled roof, running 30 yards along the wall of the Rathaus, or town hall. But the cloth weaving, dyeing, and spinning that was still a cottage industry played an increasingly important economic role in the recovery of the town from the devastation of the 1630s. The threat of poverty, however, still hung over the lives of a population vulnerable to bad weather, disease, and in some instances, unwanted pregnancies. It was also the case that the slaughtering of animals continued to take place within the city walls, a practice that would not be changed until the late nineteenth century).

In 1685, when Christian Röber married Anna Regina Fleischer, the daughter of the baker Tobias Fleischer, the groom was identified as a butcher, and the wedding was celebrated with choral singing in St Martin's Church. After the birth in 1686 of their first son (named Christian after his father), a second son named Georg was born in 1689. Oddly enough at Georg's baptism, his father Christian's surname was changed back to the spelling one encounters in Görlitz, namely Räuber.

On April 6, 1702 "at 8:00 in the evening, the butcher Röber, living on the village green found at his house doorstep a child left out in a hamper. In the hamper a cup filled with porridge and a letter were also found that indicated the child had not yet been baptized. Upon Röber's immediate notification, the baptism took place. Sponsors of the child were the clothier Apollonius Gensel, Anna Magdalene, Johann Christoph Adam's wife, and Anna Magdalena, Ernst Resch's wife."

Once again, the failure to give the first name of the butcher who was living in a house on a village green or pasture near the city walls does not allow one to know which of the many members of the family reported the foundling child. This may have been Christian (1659–1723), but it could also have been a relative since on June 6, 1707, "the butcher Michael Röber erected the first new house at the new city gate." (The original town had been built with a city wall and four gates: one facing the road to Chemnitz; a second to Wolkenstein and Annaberg; a third the Hermansdorf; and the fourth toward the Augustusburg, the elaborate hunting lodge of the Saxon rulers on the opposite side of the river and a few kilometers to the northeast. The original city wall was broken through, and the new gate erected outside the barns which stood along those walls). It seems unlikely that this "Michael" would have been the person who facilitated the emergency baptism since he would have been 73 years old by this time, but it is possible.

Nonetheless, the re-building of houses, the continued identification of the family as the purveyors of meats to the town, and being chosen to escort a visiting Russian Tsar, are all circumstances which suggest that they had survived and maintained their social and economic position in the town. The names and occupations of both spouses and godparents to children also reveal connections to the extensive spinning, weaving, and cloth-dying occupations of the community, connections that would prove a mixed blessing by the nineteenth century.

Other indications of the relative prosperity enjoyed by this family into the early decades of the eighteenth century survive in the age at death of the marriage partners, and the number of children born from marriages and surviving into adulthood. Christian (1659–1723) and his first wife Anna Regina Fleischer raised 12 children between 1686 and 1714. Christian died "suddenly" with no cause given at the beginning of August 1723 at the age of 64. His wife Anna Regina survived him until August 1729, dying at age 62.

Their second son, Georg, was not as blessed. Marrying first Anna Sophia Knödel, the daughter of the master clothier and townsman of Zschopau in 1714, this couple brought three sons into the world between 1716 and 1720. But Anna Sophia died at the beginning of March 1723 while giving birth to a fourth child who died with her. A year later on May 23, Georg married again, this time to Maria Christina Strehle, the daughter of Johann Michael Strehle, townsman and hat maker in Döbeln, who was serving as an assessor in Zschopau at the time. Seven children were born to this marriage between 1727 and 1743. Their fifth child and third son, Carl Gottlob, later identified as "the elder," was born in 1736 and his godparents included David Frantz, a clothier; Johann Christiana, the daughter of Johann Biedermann the baker; and Christian Gotthilff Gödel, the son of Gottfried, a tanner by trade. When Carl Gottlob, the youngest son of the deceased Georg, married in June of 1758, his wife Rosina Maria Klotz came from Waldkirchen. She, like her husband, was the youngest child among her siblings—her father Johann George Klotz, a farrier in that town. Of the six children born to this marriage, the oldest son, Carl Gottlob the Younger, was born in 1759 and continued in the family occupation as butcher. His godparents were Johann George Röber, a butcher as well; the wife of the butcher Christian Gottfried Röber; and Johann Christian Röber, also identified as a butcher.

It is difficult to say what lay behind this rather odd pattern of choosing godparents. Normally, the choice of godparents had, since ancient times, served the dual purpose of guaranteeing the Christian faith of the child in the hands of sponsors while also building economic and social bonds between families. The absence of any other trades, professions, or families in this particular baptism and set of sponsors therefore risked not only the violation of the laws of affinity but missed an opportunity to cultivate the social and economic connections a baptismal celebration offered. By the time Carl Gottlob was married in 1783 to Rebecca Felber of Hennersdorf, he was not only identified as a townsman and butcher of Zschopau but also as the innkeeper (*Gastwirth*) of the Zschopau *Rathaus*. Presumably, his residence in that building also enabled him to work in the butcher's stall that ran along one side of that town hall on the market square.

Historians who have traced the consequences of the Thirty Years' War for central Europe have determined that the casualties in war, the resulting famine, and loss of income cut the overall population of parts of what is now Germany in half. The 1618 population level was not restored until the late 1740s. Zschopau, like many other towns and cities within the Holy Roman Empire, appears to have been a typical victim of the conflagration. But much like the town's butcher family, the town itself substantially recovered its economic and social stability by the 1740s. However, that recovery was interrupted on October 8, 1748, when a major fire broke out, destroying St. Martin's Church, the rectory, the town school, the town hall, and many other buildings.

The fourth St. Martin's Church was dedicated on the same site as its predecessors on the first Sunday of Advent in 1751 but not until 1755 did the church celebrate the completion of the new organ. The Seven Years' War that broke out the following year in 1756 and lasting until 1763 did not bring the same degree of ruin to the towns of the Zschopau River valley. Nevertheless, the crushing defeat of the Saxon and Austrian armies by Prussia at Döbeln (a town that lay as far from Zschopau in the north as Dresden does in the east) prompted prayers for protection from the horrors of the previous century. Those horrors remained the topic of sermons which warned of the consequences for those who failed to be obedient to God and to the worldly authorities he had placed over his people.

Because service in the Saxon army would play an important but somewhat odd role in the later history of the Roeber ancestor who emigrated to North America, it is useful to recall what military service consisted of for ordinary subjects of Saxony. The Elector of Saxony decided in 1682 to form an actual army as opposed to merely local guard forces which had been the previous practice. Never renowned for military success, the Saxon army was also peculiar in that it did not recruit foreigners as Prussia did, but instead was always composed exclusively of Saxon subjects. Since the army actively recruited young men from 1682 until a draft was instituted in 1810, it is noteworthy that no member of the Röber family in or from Zschopau is mentioned as a recruit, a veteran, or having any connection with military service until the 1840s.

The battles of the Seven Years' War took place further to the north and east in Electoral Saxony, and that same pattern repeated itself during the Napoleonic Wars. In 1806—the final year of the Holy Roman Empire's existence—Saxony fought on the side of Prussia and, in suffering defeat, opened Saxony to French occupation. Three years later, Saxony fought against Austria with the Napoleonic forces but now as the Kingdom of Saxony, an elevation in status given by Napoleon. That association cost the Saxons after Napoleon's defeat. Not only was some Saxon territory awarded to victorious Prussia, but its army was re-configured to match Prussia's, a decision that provoked refusal on the part of many officers and desertion by ordinary Saxon soldiers. By the 1820s in the aftermath of Napoleon's final defeat, Saxon males were drafted to serve eight years of active duty, followed by four years in the reserves. By 1839 the active service was reduced to six years with three years of reserve duties.

The sole surviving connection between the Saxon Royal Army and the family of butchers in Zschopau occurred when on the 18th of October 1839 the 20-year-old Christian Gottlob, "a resident of Oberlungwitz" obtained, in person, a copy of his baptismal certificate from the pastor of his ancestral parish in Zschopau "for the purpose of recruitment," i.e. because he was being drafted.

Carl Gottlob the Younger, (1759–1821) the oldest son of his father of the same name and Christian Gottlob's grandfather, may have reached the height of economic and social standing enjoyed by any member of this family with his double occupation as butcher and innkeeper.

(As an aside, when Carl was nine years old, he would have known of the sudden death on August 10 of 1768 of his relative, the master butcher of the town, Johann David Röber, who "fell so unhappily in his barn that he died immediately and was buried on the 14th of that same month.")

In 1783, when he was 24 years of age, Carl Gottlob's marriage to Rebecca Felber of Hennersdorf took place while he was most probably living in the town hall itself. His wife was the only daughter of August Felber, a carpenter and cottager. Between 1783 and 1810 the couple saw the birth of four sons and a daughter before his wife's death in 1810. He was married a second time, in 1811, to Concordia Hunger, a widow, born Concordia Biedermann. Her first husband (they were married in 1804) had been the linen weaver Johann Gottfried Hunger. Carl Gottlob cared for the daughter from that first marriage (Johanne Christiane).

The eldest son from the first marriage of Carl Gottlob the Younger was Karl August (1784–1823) who died before his 40th birthday, outliving his father by only two years. When Karl August married Johanne Beata Glöckner from Hennersdorf, the wedding took place in the bride's village where her father was the *Erbrichter,* i.e. the leading man of the village administration presiding over the local court when needed, seeing that taxes were collected, and capable of passing on the post to an heir.

From this marriage seven children were born, but the declining social and economic position of the family emerges from the record of occupations and early deaths of many of that generation. The eldest child, Karl Friedrich (1809–1865), died of an inflammation of the lungs while serving as the master of Zschopau's independent handweavers—i.e. he did not become a butcher as one might have expected of the eldest son of this family. Instead, it was the second son, Friedrich Wilhelm born in 1811, who did become a butcher, marrying in 1839 and dying in 1890. The city property maps for Zschopau reveal that in 1872 the house in the *Bergstraße* belonging to Friedrich Wilhelm—identified as a butcher—had burned along with neighboring houses but was then rebuilt. Karl August's third child was Johanne Christiane, born in 1813. She never married but gave birth to an illegitimate daughter somewhere outside of Zschopau—the girl died in 1840, and she disappeared from the records. The fourth child, Christian Gottlob, was born and died on the second of September 1816. Beate Juliane, born in June of 1817, committed suicide in June of 1853 and was judged to have been mentally unbalanced. The sixth child was Christian Gottlob born on Thursday, April 1 at six p.m. His godparents included an uncle, Christian Friedrich Glöckner, a miller from Erdmannsdorf; Christiane Eleonore, the wife of David Ernst Sprung, an "inhabitant" of Waldkirchen; and Johann August Müller, "a man of property" of Kunnersdorf. The last child born to Karl August and Johanne Beate was Karl August who lived only six months. Christian Gottlob's father died when he was four years old, from consumption *(Auszehrung)*; his grandfather had died from "nerve fever" when he was two.

The collapsing fortunes of this family became even more evident by 1827 when Christian's mother Johanne Beate bore a daughter, Johanne Theresie, out of wedlock to the linen weaver Johann Ludewig. The child died within two years in 1828—the same year her paternal grandmother, Christiane Concordia, died at the age of 55 from a tumor. By 1832, Johanne Beate had now married the linen weaver Ludewig. But at some point, during this rather sad decade, Christian, the sixth child and third son of Johanne Beate and Karl August Röber, was placed as a foster-son in a town far from Zschopau—only returning at the age of 20 to obtain the copy of his baptismal certificate as he entered the Saxon Army. By the time his mother, Johanne Beate, died in 1854, Christian had left Saxony and already settled on a parcel of land in northwestern Indiana in the United States. What is not clear is why this sixth child was not apprenticed to or adopted by any of the families who had stood as his godparents at his birth. Declining economic conditions appear to provide the most likely explanation. Nothing in the surviving records in Zschopau point to a familial or an economic relationship of the Röber family to the propertied miller Carl Friedrich Uhlig of Oberhermsdorf, a town far to the west of both Zschopau and Chemnitz and closer to Zwickau where the young boy Christian Gottlob grew up learning the skills of a stocking weaver.

Surveys of the persons who held positions of political or economic influence in Zschopau through the 1820s reveal that neither butchers nor anyone from the weaving occupations or other skilled handworkers served as mayors, town councilors, recorders, local court officials, or in other offices. Nor were these positions enviable. One local historian calculated that the offices were thought to be more trouble than they were worth and were poorly paid in comparison with other Saxon cities and towns of the eighteenth and nineteenth centuries. By 1820, when the eventual emigrant Christian Gottlob was one year old, the town counted 395 linen-weavers; 140 clothiers; 65 stocking-weavers working in wool or silk; 16 trim-makers; and four dyers. Between 1802 and 1805 the first large mechanical weaving machines appeared and by the 1830s English weaving technology had displaced the old cottage industries.

Eight years before Christian Gottlob's birth, the importance of the weaving and spinning industry in Zschopau and the inadequate size and durability of earlier bridges over the Zschopau River led to the construction of a stonework bridge hailed by its completion in 1815 as an unusually impressive and graceful bridge in the Ore Mountains region. Both the surviving part of the older and the modern bridge were used by Saxon, Austrian, Russian and Prussian soldiers on the way to the Leipzig Battle of the Nations in October 1813. The new stone bridge, while aiding the rapidly industrializing spinning and weaving factories in Zschopau was also completed at the cost of the medieval burial chapel on the far side of the river, as well as much of the surrounding graveyard. As a result of this modernization, followed by the arrival of the railroad in 1861 on that same opposite side of the river where the burial chapel once stood, the graves of many families—including those of the Röbers—were destroyed.

A summary of the industrialization process in Zschopau concluded that 1818 and 1819 should be regarded as the beginning of this process. In 1802, Immanuel Gottlob Heßler had purchased land where he constructed a bleaching ground and eventually one of the largest cotton spinning factories in Saxony. In 1818, he constructed a horse-powered mechanical weaver that resulted in a mob of outraged cottagers who demanded the closure of his machine within 24 hours. The protest was put down by military force and royal officials supported Heßler's new installation. The first spinning machine began operations in Zschopau the following year. By 1836 the Bodemer factory, owned by the wealthy and powerful family that had come to dominate economic and social life in Zschopau, was re-modelled to incorporate the latest technology based on a study of the English spinning and weaving factories.

This process of industrialization would have had devastating effects upon the traditional cottage industries even under the best of economic conditions. Tragically, the displacement and impoverishment of those families who had made their living in these cloth-related trades deepened into acute crisis by the 1840s because of a succession of catastrophic crop failures and the spread of the blight that gave rise to the phenomenon known as the Potato Famine. A decade after the famine, an American amateur woman historian wrote a brief history of *Peasant Life in Germany*. Anna Johnson described the conditions in Saxony in some detail, noting that lace makers, those in the cloth-related industries and miners all lived in miserable conditions, which were especially severe among the residents of the Ore Mountains, the *Erzgebirge*.

Forty years after the crisis described by Johnson, the then-pastor of St. Martin's Church in Zschopau reflected on the miseries of his flock. He identified 1841 as Zschopau's "unlucky year" when 22 buildings were consumed by fire. Already by 1837 poverty had become so obvious in the city that a woman's society was founded in an attempt to offer aid to the indigent; by 1847 they were operating soup kitchens to prevent outright starvation among the poor. A retrospective history of the miseries of the 1840s appeared in Zschopau in 1865—an account which confirmed the observations made by Johnson and others. This "Chronicle" of Zschopau detailed the poor weather conditions beginning in the 1840s from unusually bitter winters and ice storms to summers characterized by drought and ferocious winds that beat down what crops had been planted. The poor were hard put to gather wood or to obtain bread and prices for basic necessities soared. By 1845, crop failure was followed over the next two years with no potatoes left to harvest for individual family use and only a mediocre amount of fruit.

Modern scholars have concluded that although we have more extensive knowledge of the impact of the Potato Famine on Ireland, the results of the "Potato Murrain" on the population of the European continent remain largely unknown. Even so, the work that has been published confirms the pattern—especially observations by J.C. Zadoks: "...poor harvests of potatoes, due to the same late blight, but also of grain, due to frost, drought, rust, voles, inopportune rains, floods and hailstorms. The Continental Famine was enhanced by hoarding, speculation, and poor governance. Hunger was followed by infectious diseases...the number of excess deaths due to the Continental Famine cannot yet be determined with any precision, but it clearly approaches that of the Irish Famine. The harvest failures of 1845 and 1846 and the resulting famines came on top of rural pauperization and urban discontent, and thus contributed to the revolutions of 1848 on the European Continent." Moreover, as conditions worsened through the last years of that decade, emigration to North America from the states that comprised the North German Confederation steadily increased. The figure had amounted to less than 22,000 from the beginning of the decade to 1844. By 1849, emigration increased to around 62,000 and then it exploded in the 1850s to hundreds of thousands.

The level of despair produced by these appalling conditions can be seen in the local records of towns and cities such as Zschopau. Despite the private food kitchens run by the women of St. Martin's parish, on the 8th of October 1858 "at 10 A.M. the woman from Krummhennersdorf Uhlmann engaged to the house owner and farm manager Röber threw herself into the River Zschopau." Saved from drowning, the despairing woman was judged to be insane. A year later, on the 9th of June, officials noted that "two persons have in this month committed suicide...a butcher Wilhelm Röber from here who because of the vice of drinking was already in the poorhouse hanged himself" from one of the bridges over a small brook near the town. In 1862 the master stocking-weaver Heinrich Müller also took his own life "from inability to find the means to subsist."

Two years before the worst impact of the famine made itself felt, a new pastor for St. Martin's Church arrived in Zschopau. Ludwig Wükert became famous for his social and economic engagement on behalf of the poor, a dedication that eventually led him to join the Zschopau participants in the 1848 Revolution. With his Cantor Karl Geißler, Wükert founded a mildly liberal people's political association having already joined the Gustav-Adolf Verein, the 1832 organization founded to extend aid to needy Lutheran parishes and persons both within the German states and abroad. When news of the revolutionary uprisings in Dresden, Berlin, and other major cities reached Zschopau, support for radical action accelerated. By March of 1849 a crowd of some 5,000 gathered in the town to celebrate the first-year anniversary of the outbreak of revolution. Two months later on May 4th, popular pressure on the local provisional town government resulted in 95 men of the town marching to Dresden to strengthen the revolutionary barricades in the Saxon capital. Three days later, the church Cantor Geißler led another 300 men to Dresden. On May 13, however, a combined Prussian and Saxon military force entered Zschopau, and a detail entered the Church as Pastor Würkert was preaching. Arrested after he had finished his sermon, Würkert was taken into custody along with Geißler and 63 other townsmen. Among those arrested were Karl Gustav and Karl Heinrich Röber, both identified as journeymen weavers. Kept in the Augustusburg castle, Würkert was subsequently imprisoned in Waldheim from 1851 to 1854 before being pardoned. He never returned to a pastorate, moving instead to Leipzig where he opened the Hotel de Saxe and continued to give political speeches before retiring to his hometown of Leisnig, where he published the newspaper the *Free Bell* before dying there in 1876.

The radicalization of those members of this family who had, since the beginning of the 19th century, become dependent upon the cloth and spinning trades hardly surprises anyone who has read the harrowing accounts of impoverishment suffered by the 1840s. Stories of farmers found dead in their fields and of people reduced to eating boiled nettles, grasses, or already-infected potatoes with the resulting explosion of typhus, tuberculosis, dysentery, and cholera—all have been documented for various parts of Europe. The inadequacy of private relief efforts had been recognized by pastors possessed of a social conscience who concluded that nothing less than a change in the political regimes of Europe would address the economic and social evils they and their congregations suffered. This radicalization never left Zschopau and, as later events in the 20th century would prove, would involve the remaining members of the Röber family in Zschopau in confrontation with the National Socialist Regime by the mid-1930s.

How the young Christian Gottlob managed to survive the horrors of the famine may have been due to his having been drafted into the Saxon Royal Army in 1839. At the least, soldiers were guaranteed food, clothing, and a place to sleep, all advantages that would have warded off the worst impacts of the deepening famine of the mid-1840s. Still, puzzles surround this later emigrant's early years. Drafted in 1839, Christian should have been still on active duty in 1845 when his six-year term of service ended. Instead, on July 7, 1844 after banns *[of matrimony]* had been read on three successive Sundays in both Zschopau and in Oberlungwitz—the respective baptismal parishes, the pastor of St. Martin's Church in Oberlungwitz recorded the marriage of: "Master Christian Gottlob Roeber, resident and stocking weaver here, second legitimate son of Master Carl August Röber, citizen and butcher in Zschopau and foster son of Master Carl Friedrich Uhlig, miller in Oberhermsdorf, to Bertha Ulrich, only legitimate daughter of Master Daniel Friedrich Ulrich, houseowner and stocking-maker in Oberlungwitz." The marriage was performed "in der Stille," i.e. as a private ceremony, and not "as is customary" (*gewöhnlich*), that is in a more formal setting, perhaps with singing and the use of the organ.

In her old age in America, Bertha told her daughter that she was born in Oberlungwitz and was the daughter of a prosperous family. If her father Daniel Friedrich owned his own home, as the records indicate, Bertha's memory, at least relatively speaking, was correct. In other records he is identified as not only a stocking-weaver but a *Strumpfaktor*, i.e. he was either the foreman for a larger weaving group, or in charge of exporting the finished stockings in trade to the larger market to Chemnitz some 15 kilometers to the East. In other entries, however, he is identified as a *Strumpffabrikant*, indicating that perhaps as many as three weaving looms were active within the house that he owned. Although Christian Röber's foster-father Carl Friedrich Uhlig had settled as a miller in Oberhermsdorf, a nearby village of some 70 persons, Johann Emmanuel Samuel Uhlig had been one of the founders of the first stocking-weavers' groups active in Oberlungwitz since 1731. The town's origins can be traced back to Benedictine missionary monks who settled in the area between 1100 and 1150. Ultimately, their chapel grew into St. Martin's Church which boasted a tower by 1452. As was the case in Zschopau, the town was plundered during the Thirty Years' War and suffered through the plague years of 1633-39. By the 1750s, the master weavers of the town formed the first trade guild. By the 1830s, the industrial face of the village was apparent when the weavers formed their own guild group in 1838, by which time the 200 weaving masters presided over a larger group of journeymen and apprentices.

Exactly when and how the young Christian Gottlob found his way from Oberhermsdorf to the larger town to learn the skills of a stocking-weaver remains uncertain. Since he returned from military service at age 25 to marry the 19-year-old Bertha Ulrich in Oberlungwitz, he may have learned his trade in that house from his future father-in-law. Since he was identified as a *Meister Strumpfwirker,* that title indicates he had risen to a high level of skill in his learned trade. Why the relatively prosperous Daniel Friedrich and his wife Helene Dorothea would have agreed to marry their only daughter to a young man who—despite his being a master weaver—owned no property and faced uncertain future prospects as the economic crisis of the 1840s deepened is also unclear. Daniel Friedrich and Helene also had a son, Reinhold, born in 1827, two years after his sister Bertha. Reinhold naturally would have been the presumed heir and successor in his father's trade. He would go on to marry well to Caroline Friederike Thierfelder of Stollberg, whose father Friedrich Traugott was the superintendent of the local church home for the sick and elderly.

The possible explanation for the date of Christian's and Bertha's wedding, however, appears in the recording of the birth of their child Heinrich Louis on September 1, 1844, two months after the marriage. By the time the child was born, his parents were residents in the small village of Gersdorf, only a few kilometers distant from Oberlungwitz. Christian was by that time working as a stocking-weaver, possibly in conjunction with one of the town's other masters, although which master is not clear. Christian Gottlieb Hillig had founded a stocking-weaving concern in 1829 and by 1846 Carl Friedrich Schneider had opened a second. A general, although brief, period of modest prosperity was encompassed between those two dates—by 1832 a second school for children opened in the town and by 1839 Gersdorf boasted its own civic administration. But the 1844 birth of Heinrich Louis brought only sorrow to his parents. On November 25th at 7:30 in the evening, the pastor of St. Mary's church in Gersdorf buried the "only and legitimate child," two months and 26 days old, a victim of a seizure *(Schlagfluß)*—possibly apoplexy or epilepsy, or an attack brought on by high fever.

The town of Gersdorf counted about 1,887 inhabitants when Christian and Bertha settled there. By 1846, the stocking-weavers of the town founded their own guild. Unlike Oberlungwitz, Gersdorf's political history had been tied to the history of the territories belonging to the powerful house of Schönburg whose hereditary lands by the nineteenth century were being integrated into royal Saxony. The Counts von Schönburg-Waldenburg had governed from the town of Lichtenstein about 22 kilometers west of Chemnitz. Prior to the founding of their own guild, the stocking-weavers of Gersdorf had been obligated to operate under the guild in the larger town and to supply wares to that administrative center. As the famine deepened and the economy collapsed, the reputation of Count Otto Viktor I von Waldenburg as a compassionate ruler who declined to demand all of the rents and contributions owed to him by tenants did not suffice. As revolution broke out in Dresden in May of 1848 a sympathetic group of men from Gersdorf joined a larger crowd from the surrounding area and attacked the von Waldenburg castle in Lichtenstein, burning it to the ground. Anyone familiar with the poet Heinrich Heine's famous 1844 work *Die armen Weber* (the poor weavers) recalls Heine's ominous threat put into the mouths of the starving Silesians who warn that they are weaving the burial shroud of Germany. The poem's indictment of the Prussian-Silesian oaths of loyalty to God, King, and Fatherland extended beyond Silesia and Saxony as well.

If Christian Röber harbored any sympathies for the radical political activity of his fellow residents in Gersdorf, he kept them to himself. His choice of names for his sons gives no hint of political leanings, nor of intentions to use familiar family names. His son Heinrich Louis's first name might have reflected the use of the name Heinrich by various counts of the Schönburg ruling house, but the name was never used in the Roeber family nor by Bertha Ulrich's family. Nor was the name Louis. The names of Christian and Bertha's second son, born 21 September 1845 as Clemens Theodore, present a similar puzzle. Members of the Catholic Wettin dynasty in Dresden numbered a Clemens Wenceslaus (1739–1803) and Clemens Maria (1798–1822) but these men seem unlikely candidates as models for Lutheran villagers of Gersdorf. The name Theodore also reflects no ancestral ties to either of the parental families. When the young Clemens Theodore was baptized on October 2nd his sponsors included Wilhelm Friedrich Frank, a stocking-weaver and house owner in Oberlungwitz; Chrstina Concordia Uhlig, his grandmother; and Reinhold Ulrich, his uncle, by now a householder in Oberlungwitz.

The two-year old Theodore was joined by a younger sister, Augusta Hedwig, in March 1847. Her grandmother Helene Dorothea served as her baptismal sponsor along with Christian Röber's stepfather Carl Friedrich Uhlig and Augusta Hedwig Schindler, the wife of Carl Gottlieb Schindler, a stocking-weaver resident in Oberlungwitz. Three years later on February 25, 1850, Hedwig Bertha became the second daughter and fourth child born to Christian and Bertha. Her grandfather Friedrich Daniel Ulrich, her uncle Reinhold, and the owner of a bleaching ground in Herrndorf Christian Gottlieb Huld served as her sponsors. At some point during the next calendar year, Christian Röber made the decision to leave his family in Gersdorf and to emigrate alone to the United States.

The normal procedure for those desiring to leave their homeland involved filing for a permit with the Saxon authorities. Unfortunately, the regional records that would have been kept at Lichtenstein for the area, including Gersdorf, appear to have been lost. Whether Christian actually was able to demonstrate that he was debt-free and could pay the administrative fees that varied between 5 to 10 per cent of his property cannot be determined. The property listings for Gersdorf do not show him ever having owned real estate in the town. Given the dire circumstances many Saxons in both cities and countryside continued to suffer, he may have been exempted in exchange for proving that he could leave some means for Bertha and his children to survive in his absence. Before he left Gersdorf for the last time, however, Christian was present for the birth and baptism of his third daughter, the fifth child Anna Maria, born and baptized on January 25, 1852. Once again, Grandmother Helene Dorothea Ulrich stood as sponsor along with Carolina Ulrich, the child's aunt by marriage to Reinhold Ulrich, and Carl Gottlob Schindler, another stocking-weaver. But like Christian and Bertha's first son Heinrich Louis, Anna Maria would die before this family was re-united in North America.

Emigration from the region of Saxony in which this family lived involved choosing between two means of reaching the ports where emigrants could take ship. For some, taking a riverboat on the Elbe River would bring them to Hamburg, the main departure port supervised by the Office for Proof of Emigrants. In 1850, Hamburg authorities had founded the "Association for the Protection of Emigrants" that sought to house emigrants in licensed hostels while they waited to board ship. The Atlantic crossing by the early 1850s was beginning to change dramatically. In 1838 the crossing by the "Great Western" combined wooden sail and paddle wheel ship took fifteen and a half days. The first true steamship left Hamburg in 1850 and, increasingly, steamers with iron hulls and screw propulsion plus sails would cut the crossing time by 1860 to between eight to nine days. For the poor, however, the trek from Saxony to Hamburg—over 250 miles—meant walking for days or, if they could afford it, riding in horse-drawn coach. The railroad connected Dresden, Chemnitz, and Leipzig to Hamburg by rail by the 1850s and most emigrants began arriving in Hamburg by train. It is most likely that Christian took a sailing ship whose average crossing time amounted to around 43 days since as late as 1856 only five percent of emigrants landing in New York arrived by steamship. Christian's ship the *Perseverance* out of Hamburg docked in New York on June 10, 1852, which suggests that he had left Gersdorf in April, as soon as weather conditions allowed the long journey north to Hamburg. The record of his arrival identified him as age 33, occupation unknown, "destination Illinois."

Authorities in the German states had, as early as the seventeenth century, attempted to control or suppress agents circulating broadsides and advertisements urging emigration. The Saxon parliament *(Landtag)* in 1848 issued a new law forbidding the spread of information to promote emigration, to no effect. Saxons knew of, and preferred the midwestern states of Illinois, Indiana, Ohio, Wisconsin, and Missouri above all others. Either rumor conveyed by word-of-mouth, or actual notices circulated as handbills must have alerted Christian to the possibility of acquiring property in the midwestern United States.

One other tantalizing, but inconclusive piece of evidence suggests that by the early nineteenth century, emigration from Zschopau to the United States had already been pioneered by another member of the Roeber family. Among the surviving record of cases brought before the Royal Saxon Court of Zschopau, two volumes of papers document the disposition of property left by Friedrich Gotthard Röber of Zschopau—an owner of property in the city but no longer a resident, having emigrated to America by the time of the court action (1851–53). What connection this member of the family had to the later emigrant Christian also remains unclear. But the awareness of emigration from Zschopau to North America may have played some part in Christian's decision to seek economic and social survival in America at the very time his relative's property in Zschopau was being disposed of.

Upon Christian Gottlob's arrival in New York, he joined other migrants who boarded trains bound for the rapidly expanding city of Chicago on the southwestern shores of Lake Michigan. The details of his first years in America have been lost, and no certain memories of those years found their way into later family accounts that can be tied to public or private written evidence. According to oral family history, he found work as a day laborer in Chicago. Whether he was able to communicate with his wife and family in Gersdorf between 1852 and 1854 seems unlikely given the harrowing events that now began to occur in the family he left behind—a family which struggled to survive without him.

As a widower in his final years, Christian's son Theodore Roeber sometimes reminisced, between 1913 and 1916, about his childhood. At those times, he darned his stockings while chatting with his new daughter-in-law, Fannie Alderson Roeber. The memories were grim. Theodore walked on deformed feet, the result of having no shoes as a child and having suffered from acute frostbite. He remembered being so ashamed of his lack of clothing that he would run into the woods surrounding Gersdorf to avoid being seen when the carriages and horses of the well-to-do came through the main street that connected Gersdorf to the neighboring villages and to Chemnitz in the east, or Lichtenstein in the west. The cultivation of potatoes around Gersdorf had failed in the years right after his birth, and although he did not suffer starvation, he was only of average height for European males of that time, even as a grown man, five feet five inches tall. As a child, Theodore must have received a good grounding in basic literacy since he wrote well in both German and a passable English. But his family life in those challenging years became the subject of later, bitter controversy. The most striking evidence for this is the absence in Gersdorf and Oberlungwitz church records of any mention of the events that then occurred in Christian and Bertha's family.

Between 1853 and 1857 three more children were born to Bertha: Oskar, in 1853; Hulda, in April 1857; and Maria, born just before Bertha arrived in New York on October 23, 1857. Bertha was accompanied by her older daughters, Augusta and Bertha, and the younger children, all traveling on the ship *Jason* out of Bremen and Southampton. Why Bertha did not follow her husband's route via Hamburg is unclear; although, by the mid-1850s, Bremerhaven offered a port of emigration further to the west than Hamburg and thus, perhaps this meant a slightly shorter journey from Saxony.

Her son, Clemens Theodore, had pioneered this route first. The eleven-year-old boy had arrived in New York on April 14, 1856, a cabin passenger aboard the U.S. Mail Steamer *Washington* from Bremen. The church records in Gersdorf reveal that on March 5, 1856, eleven-year-old Clemens Theodore obtained a copy of his baptismal certificate from the pastor of St. Mary's Church in Gersdorf before setting out—alone—to join his father in America. That entry stands as the final evidence of Christian and Bertha's family presence in Saxony.

However, earlier records relating to and subsequent records failing to document baptisms offer evidence of turmoil in Christian and Bertha's family. Prior to emigrating, in 1849 Christian had been asked to serve as godfather to his brother-in-law Reinhold's second child Maria Helene. But at no time did Bertha appear as a sponsor, neither in 1849, nor again when Reinhold's son Robert was baptized in 1853, nor at Paul's baptism in 1855. No record of the birth or the baptism of two of the three youngest of Bertha's children exists in either Gersdorf or Oberlungwitz. Nor is there a record of a second marriage of Bertha to another man. Although illegitimacy was frowned on by both Catholic and Protestant churches, care was always taken to baptize such children, as had been the case of the foundling left on the doorstep of the unnamed Roeber, the Zschopau butcher, in 1702.

Although no written records survive, an oral tradition in the family stated that Christian in 1854 sent for his family to join him in America. (This oral tradition was cited in an Indiana court case during the 1920s—more on this later.) According to the family's oral tradition, Bertha replied that she could not come because she had given birth to younger children by another man. Nevertheless, Christian insisted that she bring all the children with her and join him in Indiana where he now possessed his own land—a feat that he would never have accomplished had he remained in Saxony.

Born in 1819 and sent away as a young child from his family in Zschopau, Christian had learned the skills of a stocking-weaver during the decades of industrialization that destroyed the cottage weavers' groups of which he had been a member and into whose ranks he had also married. Within two years of his arrival in Chicago, he would, by January 1854, become the purchaser of three parcels of land on the border between Indiana and Illinois on the Little Calumet River. It was there that his son Theodore joined him in 1856, as did the rest of his family in the autumn of 1857, including three children he had not fathered. Since Christian had arrived in 1852, he became eligible for citizenship in the same year that his wife and her children arrived in America—Bertha was also granted citizenship.

(The naturalization laws of the United States had originally, in 1790, required only a two-year residency before the applicant could become a citizen. Spurred by fears of the radical implications of the French Revolution, the American Congress in 1795 increased the residency requirement to five years where it has remained ever since. In 1855—one year after Christian's property purchase, the law was altered so that alien wives were automatically granted citizenship of their U.S. citizen husbands.)

Christian's reunion with his family lasted approximately two years. He was found dead in his fields in December 1859. His nine-year-old daughter, Hedwig Bertha, kept wake over his body but no record of a funeral, or a place of burial has survived. The cultivation, and eventual disposition of Christian's land in Indiana now passed to his widow, and to his sole surviving son, fourteen-year-old Theodore. Perhaps out of a sense of filial loyalty to his deceased father, Theodore intended to preserve Christian's property intact for his father's legitimate children. Theodore appears to have harbored understandably bitter memories of his childhood. Nor was his relationship with his mother one that revealed much understanding or sympathy for her desperate efforts to survive in the absence of her husband and in the face of grinding poverty and isolation. These strained familial relationships and memories of life on the social margins in the Ore Mountains of Saxony were destined to shape the subsequent struggle of these emigrants to find their place in the American experiment.

Sources

Personal conversation and correspondence with Pastor Klaus Roeber of Berlin in Herrnhut, Germany, 2007–08.

Rudolph Zaunick, *Acta Historica Leopoldina: Der Dresdner Stadtphysikus Friedrich August Röber (1765–1827)* (Leipzig: Johann Ambrosius Barth Verlag, 1966).

Das Mittlere Zschopaugebiet (Berlin: Akademie-Verlag, 1977), 156-62.

Neue Sächsische Kirchengalerie: Die Parochie Zschopau (Leipzig: Arwed Strauch, 1901).

Zschopau: Alte Stadt im Erzgebirge (Horb am Neckar: Geiger-Verlag, 1992).

Anna C. Johnson, *Peasant Life in Germany* (New York: Charles Scriber, 1859).

Dr. Weinhold, *Chronik von Zschopau und Umgegend: Teilweise nach amtlichen Berichten zusammengestellt und herausgegeben* (Zschopau, 1865).

Genealogy and Property owned or rented, Correspondence and Files courtesy of Hermann von Strauch, retired Organist and Kantor of St. Martin's Church, Zschopau, 1983–1996.

Parish records of St. Martin's Church of Oberlungwitz and St. Mary's Church, Gersdorf.

J.C. Zadoks. "The Potato Murrain on the European Continent and the Revolutions of 1848," *Potato Research* (2008), 51:5-45.

Ira A. Glazier and P. William Filby, eds., *Germans to America: Lists of Passengers Arriving at U.S. Ports,* 24 vols (1850–1870); Vol. 3: p.48 Christian Raber age 33 arrived New York, destination Illinois on ship *Perseverance* out of Hamburg, 10 June 1852; Vol. 11 p.394, Rober, Bertha, 32, Augusta, 9, Bertha, 7, Oscar, 4, Hilda, ½ year old from Saxony arriving on ship *Jason* out of Bremen and Southampton, in New York 23 October 1857.

National Archives, Ship Passenger Lists Microfilm Roll 161 no. 219 Bremen to New York 14 April 1856: US Mail Steamer "Washington" person #23 Roeber, Theodore, age 10—boy, born Germany, to U.S. as cabin passenger.

Correspondence and Genealogy charts, Martin Mak, to author, 1978–1986.

Andrea Bentschneider, "From Saxony to the New World: Emigration in the 19th Century," at https://www.beyond-history.com

Royal Saxon Court of Zschopau Act 32997 #90 (On Friedrich Gotthard Roeber of Zschopau emigrated before 1851).

Johann Karl Seidemann, *Die Unruhen im Erzgebirge während des deutschen Bauernkriegs nach den Acten des königlich Sächsischen Hauptstaats-Archiv zu Dresden* (München: Verlag der Akademie 1865), 148-204.

Chapter Two

Farmers, Veterans, and the American West

On September 28, 1850, the Congress of the United States approved an act "to enable the state of Arkansas and other states to reclaim the 'swamp lands' within their limits." This act donated Federal lands not only to the State of Arkansas but also those held within the state of Indiana. That state was now authorized to offer "swamp and overflowed lands" to interested buyers. By May 29, 1852, the legislature of Indiana had accepted this donation of lands from the Federal government and enabled those willing to drain and reclaim these areas to do so by paying a minimum price of $1.25 per acre. On January 17, 1854, a warranty deed for 127.8 acres of land was given to "Christian G. Roberts" who paid $159.75 for the property that lay on the boundary of Illinois and Indiana and along the Little Calumet River. As later corrections admitted, the purchaser was not "Christian Roberts" but Christian G. Röber.

Various groups of the First Peoples of North America were familiar with these swamplands, hunting in the swamps and sloughs that teemed with mink, muskrat, fish, and aquatic fowl, along with cranberries and huckleberries. But none ever settled in the area. At one time, the Potawatomi Tribe had used the area as a hunting ground, but between the 1826 Treaty of Mississinewa and the Treaty of Tippecanoe in 1832, the Potawatomi relinquished their lands in northwestern Indiana, although some still visited the region and traded both furs and berries with settlers. The Calumet Beach Trail ran along a ridge south of the Little Calumet River from east to west. It was one of several routes which the Sauk, Potawatomi, and other First People Nations had used to traverse a swampy region—journeys that were dangerous for those seeking to cross it.

By May 1852 the future of this region changed dramatically when the Michigan Central Railroad managed to arrange an agreement with the Illinois Central that brought Chicago into the network of existing rail connections to the east along the Great Lakes. Whether Christian Röber, arriving as he did in New York in June of 1852 was able to reach Chicago by means of this connection remains unknown. Neither can we document his first years in the United States. Oral history and memory in the family recalls him finding work as a day laborer in Chicago itself.

At some point, having arrived in Illinois, he became aware of a German-speaking settlement in neighboring northwest Indiana. A mile south of Gibson Station on the Michigan Central Railroad, the small community known as Hessville began to emerge, founded by Joseph Hess in 1851. Hess served as the postmaster of this town as well as the proprietor of the general store. Hess had emigrated from Alsace-Lorraine and therefore spoke a very different version of German from the group of farmers, trappers, carpenters and blacksmiths who settled a few miles further to the west in a region that became known as "Saxony." It was in this area that Christian Röber bought his land. Perhaps he was attracted to the spot because it was occupied by other immigrants who would have spoken the Saxon dialect of his homeland, although nothing in his personal or family background would have prepared him for the life of a farmer.

The first schoolhouse in Hessville was built too late to have been of use to Christian or his son Theodore. However, the school became a benchmark of the continuing growth of the "Saxony" District (later known as Woodmar). Between the school's initial construction in 1869 and the 1880s, a second story was added to the schoolhouse where a German-speaking teacher hired by the Saxony parents taught children in the German language.

Most of what can be reconstructed about the history of the Roeber family and their neighbors in this region between 1854 and 1876 comes from a court case that was reported in detail in the *Lake County Times* and the *Hammond Indiana Times* on December 3, 1926. Headlines warned that "Suit May Cloud Title to Hammond Land Worth Million Dollars" noting that the seventy acres of highly valuable property affecting "Hammond's Finest Residence District" was now the basis of a case in the Superior Court which would probably provide employment for most of Indiana's legal profession. Begun in November of 1926 in Lake Superior Court, the case went through the Porter County Circuit Court and the Appellate Court of Indiana until November of 1928. In the end, the court ruled that the plaintiffs in the case had waited too long to contest the division of the original property purchased by Christian Roeber in 1854. The statute of limitations and adverse possession meant that claims made by the descendants of Bertha Roeber's three youngest children, Oskar, Hulda, and Maria to a share in the division of Christian Roeber's property could not be sustained. But in the testimony of those called before the courts, the earliest years of the immigrant and his family emerged, although with some differences in the memories of what had taken place, memories that included those of Bertha's daughter Mary (married surname Mak), the last surviving child who was then 70 years old, as well as Christian and Bertha's grandchildren.

The original house which Christian had constructed stood just north of the Little Calumet River with a western border located on the state line dividing Indiana from Illinois. The area was one of dense woods and water, with prairie land extending east toward the town of Hessville.

The surviving accounts, kept by Joseph Hess at his general store, show that Christian was one of his customers. Upon Christian's death, Hess submitted his account for the deceased "Dader *[debtor]* to me Joseph Hess in the Sum of five Dollars five Sents *[cents]* for Groceries had during the year 1858." But Christian also had an account in Blue Island, Illinois where at the time of his death on 1 December 1859 he owed $4.41 to a storekeeper named Butler.

Also, another account with William Baumbach's store, which came to light after probate in January, revealed that, as of February of 1860, Christian had purchased a linen coat, a boy's hat, trimmings for a boy's coat and vest, and 3¾ yards of "Cassimer." (This cloth, originally made from Spanish merino sheep's wool, had become known in England as Kerseymere and by the nineteenth century was now made of cotton, wool, or mohair wool which was woven into a fabric commonly used for making suits for men and boys.) Christian had owed Baumbach $9.19 on account. Of that amount, Baumbach received $1.50 in January of that year when Christian's estate was probated.

A.H. Brass also submitted his bill for $5.00 for making a coffin and burying the late Christian, charging an additional $1.00 for digging the grave and noting that the costs of a pound of coffee (sixteen cents) and a pound of flour (twenty-seven cents) were also due him. The personal property for Christian (who had died intestate without a will) was appraised by A.H. Brass and W.L. Vanstenburgh who found that Christian's personal property amounted to $195.00 but that he had died still owing a total of $48.48. The administrator of the estate, Chauncey Wilson, estimated for the Lake County court that the real estate owned by Christian, some 107.80 acres, was worth $1,200.00 and he asked the court for an order to sell as much of the real estate "as may be necessary to pay the debts."

A closer look at the actual inventory revealed that Christian had loaned $5.00 to an "F. Albert." Lake County court records also showed that as of 12 September 1859 he had sold to James Hope the northernmost 20 acres of the original 127.8 acres he had purchased in 1854. This transaction still left a sizeable farm situated north of the Little Calumet River, ranging from section 13 in the south to section 12 in the north. The personal effects in the household were modest but included a bed and bedstead, cupboard ware, a churn, carpenter's tools, 1.25 bushels of beans, flour barrels, wooden bowls and tubs, and two dozen pans. The farm itself included a yoke of oxen and harness, a lumber wagon, four cows, three yearlings, two calves, five tons of hay, a plough, a dray *[a strong cart or wagon]*, "downed wood on the premises," two pitchforks, 25 head of poultry, three hoes, a hay knife, and a scythe.

Inflation calculators set the value of $1.00 in 1860 to be worth $32.96 in 2021. This means the $159.75 paid for 127.8 acres in 1854 would be worth approximately $5,265.36 in twenty-first century money. But neither Christian nor his son Theodore would ever reap an immediate cash payment for sale of property, in Indiana, or later, in Kansas which might have been applied to their land purchases in western Colorado. A more useful way of understanding Christian's "worth" at the time of his death emerges if we consider what he paid for basic foodstuffs—the bill for a pound of coffee brewed perhaps as part of a wake charged by A.H. Brass amounting to 16 cents and a pound of flour costing 17 cents. Compared with the poverty and actual starvation which Christian had witnessed in Saxony in the 1840s, he had managed to become a modest property owner. However, he did not live long enough to enjoy the acquisition of a precarious hold on a circumstance of middling status and the reunion of his family.

Controversy and some degree of ill will apparently existed between Christian's widow Bertha and their oldest son Theodore. Theodore later told his daughter-in-law, Fannie Alderson Roeber, that he had ruined the suit of clothes his father had bought for him as a boy. This occurred either while his father was still alive, or perhaps sometime between 1860 and 1865. As punishment, Theodore was made to kneel on a floor covered in dried peas.

The circumstances surrounding the family in the late 1860s included somewhat conflicting recollections. Some who testified in the 1926 court case recalled that all of the children lived with Christian and Bertha in the original homestead. Others remembered that, at least initially, Bertha lived apart with the Steinbach family whose son Nicholas would later marry her daughter Augusta. Christian being found dead in his fields in December 1859 also produced dark rumors. Some said he had been gored by one of the team of oxen he was working. Others gossiped that Bertha had conspired to have him killed. No one remembered Bertha keeping wake for her husband, but Mary Mak, the youngest of Bertha's children did remember that she had been told that her half-sister Hedwig Bertha, Christian's second daughter, kept wake over her father. If so, Hedwig Bertha—who was born in February and baptized in March of 1850 in Gersdorf—would at that time have been a young girl of only nine years old.

No Lutheran pastor cared for the German-speakers of the "Saxony" area and no funeral was held for which we have a record, but perhaps the coffee and flour bill charged by A.H. Brass along with his expenses for making

Christian's coffin and digging the grave indicated some form of a wake. It is possible that Christian was buried in what became the North Township cemetery in Hessville—a location which was a mile or more to the east of his property. However, by the time an inventory of old graves was made there in 1957, many vintage gravestones had either no names on them or had weathered so badly that they could not be read. If Christian was buried there, or on his own property, no mention was made of this by later descendants.

The 1860 Federal Census listed Bertha and her six children as residents on the original farm—but it also noted the presence of two farm laborers, Fiedile and Johanna Heckelman, 36 and 14 years of age, respectively. During the next five years, the Roeber name and that of Heckelman would now play a significant role in the later history of the Roeber family. Christian H. Heckelman—whose original name in Europe was more probably Deckelman—had been born in 1824 in Hesse-Darmstadt, a year before Bertha Ulrich Roeber. In early September 1865, Bertha brought a lawsuit in the Lake County Court of Common Pleas against her six children, asking for a partition of Christian's lands so that she could claim an undivided third part of the property, with the children each to receive a sixth of the remaining two-thirds. One of the commissioners subpoenaed and appointed by the court was Christian Heckelman. The children had been summoned in July to answer Bertha's partition claim. Alexander McDonald was appointed guardian to the minor heirs, but there was no contestation of Bertha's claim, and the court ordered the partition of the property as she had asked.

A few years later, Bertha Roeber married Christian Heckelman on January 25, 1868. Six children were born to this couple in what appears to have been a problematic relationship. The 1870 Census showed nine children living with Christian and Bertha—Oskar, Hulda, and Maria who had been conceived out of wedlock in Gersdorf between 1854 and 1858—and six children ranging from ages seven to one, born between 1862 and 1869.

Christian and Bertha divorced on February 21, 1876, and Heckelman later died in 1881. In letters Theodore received in Hanover, Kansas, from relatives and friends in Indiana, he learned that the man referred to only as "the Heckelman" *("der Heckelman")* had died, and that he had not been living with Bertha at the time.

Even after Heckelman's departure, Bertha had remained on the original property in Indiana. But after a fire broke out that destroyed the original home and its contents in 1873, Bertha sold her portion of Christian's property and moved to live with her youngest children, including her son Oscar. Oscar, along with many others, found employment in the burgeoning meat-packing town of Hammond that was then expanding and would, by the early 20th century, annex Hessville, Saxony, and the original Roeber farmland.

One of the correspondents who informed Theodore of Heckelman's demise was his best friend and later brother-in-law, Franz Planer. Born in 1844, a year before Theodore himself, Planer and his family had arrived in the "Saxony" area of northwest Indiana by the 1860s. He would marry Theodore's younger sister, Hedwig Bertha, on May 20, 1870.

When Theodore moved west, Planer's son William would eventually make the long journey by train to visit Theodore on the latter's ranch in western Colorado, and Theodore made repeated trips to Indiana to visit the Planers. Planer maintained life-long contact with his brother-in-law until Theodore's death in 1916.

The first photographic records of the Roeber family in America include two images of Bertha, taken when she was living in Hammond, Indiana, probably in the 1880s. A third photograph pictures Theodore and Franz Planer shortly before they both enlisted in D Company of the Ninth Regiment Illinois Volunteer Cavalry at Niles, Illinois, on February 23, 1865. Planer would remain in the service until mustered out on October 31, 1865, when the Cavalry was disbanded. Theodore's enlistment, however, lasted only four months. He was mustered out in June because of disability, having contracted "asthma" and "lung disease" on picket duty in cold rain during the Cavalry's campaign in Mississippi. After a battle at Nashville, Tennessee, in January of 1865, the Union troops were to have been sent to Huntsville, Alabama. Instead of that planned campaign, the 9th Illinois had been diverted to Eastport, Mississippi, and the troops had remained there throughout the spring months, through the assassination of Abraham Lincoln.

By 1880, Theodore decided to make application for a disability pension. In 1882, seeking to have the pension amount increased, he contacted those who could testify on his behalf. These witnesses included Heinrich Lühring, who had returned from Kansas to visit in Indiana. Lühring testified that while visiting in January and February of 1872 he had found Theodore "sick, suffering from Asthma the same as when he arrived in Kansas in the year 1876 and lived with me." Julius Holstein, now living in Minnesota swore that he had known Theodore who "was a neighbor" known to Holstein "for twenty-four years, and from his twelfth year and prior to and at date of his enlistment in said service. . .knows he was a sound healthy able-bodied man, particularly that he was free from asthma and disease of lungs. . .never sick until his enlistment." The recruit was described as having grey eyes, light hair, five feet five inches high, and as a petitioner for a pension someone who had been first employed as a "laborer" then as a "farmer" and "clerk."

When he began his pursuit of a pension, Theodore had contacted the former captain of his Company D and received a letter from Patrick Kelly now living in Toledo, Ohio. In that January 1881 letter Kelly wrote: "I am glad to hear that you are prosecuting a claim for pension. You have contracted disease while in the line of your duty defending the old flag, long may she wave. I think this plank *[i.e., an important form which may have attached to the letter]* is filled out all right as it was done by the Clerk of the Court himself with his official signature signed to it himself." Although "asthma" is cited in the documentary evidence, it is more likely that Theodore contracted some form of chronic bronchial bacterial or fungal infection which, absent the later discovery and use of antibiotics until well after his death, was never correctly diagnosed or treated.

Theodore had returned from his brief service in the Grand Army of the Republic (GAR) as a 19-year-old; he would not reach his age of majority until 29 September 1866 and was therefore still a minor when his father's land had been partitioned at his mother's request earlier that month. He had been identified as a "laborer" at the time of his enlistment and presumably he resumed work on the family property. As the oldest legitimate male heir of his father, Theodore apparently harbored considerable resentment over the decisions his mother and Christian Heckelman had made, a resentment that became clear five years later when he himself would begin a court case to ensure that his mother's three illegitimate children *would not inherit* his father's property.

At some point between his return to Indiana in September of 1865 and December of 1868, Theodore met a young woman whose German accent revealed her family's background from Linden-Uelzen, a village in the Kingdom of Hannover, about 54 miles northeast of the royal capital. Her father, Heinrich Lühring, was born in 1818 and would live until 1894. Heinrich married Katherine Maria Müller who was three years his junior but who pre-deceased him in 1886. Five children were born to this marriage; Maria Dorothea, who later caught Theodore's eye, had been born on September 27, 1848, and was the second oldest.

The *chain migration* pattern that was a long-established custom among immigrant families was also the case here. Heinrich emigrated in 1866 with his second child Maria, leaving his eldest son, his wife, and two younger daughters in Hanover. Finding work as a day laborer in Chicago, Heinrich settled in the "Saxony" area of Lake County while his daughter, Maria Dorothea, worked as a maid for a family in Chicago. The balance of the family joined Heinrich and Maria in 1867. But, perhaps seeking a community where their way of speaking German was more prominent, Heinrich and Katherine Maria moved with most of their children to northeastern Kansas. Their daughter, Maria Dorothea, according to at least one family memory, met Theodore Roeber when he had attended a picnic to which they had both been invited.

Recalling the event later to his daughter-in-law, Theodore had discovered that the man who had escorted Maria Dorothea to the event had abandoned her for another woman. Theodore offered to see the young woman home safely and began to court her shortly thereafter. Another family memory of their meeting had her working either in Chicago or a neighboring area of Illinois where she was employed to shuck oysters. Both stories are perhaps plausible. The connections to towns, stores, and a marriage in Illinois became even more obvious when Clemens Theodore Roeber and Maria Dorthea Lühring were married on 23 December 1868. The couple secured a marriage license at Crown Point in Lake County, Indiana, but they were married in a

Lutheran ceremony in Dolton, Illinois, only a few miles west of the Roeber homestead. Since Theodore's father had also worked in Chicago, and had store accounts in Blue Island, Illinois, those connections may account for the otherwise somewhat odd decision of both Theodore and his friend Franz Planer to join an Illinois volunteer cavalry unit rather than one in Indiana.

As subsequent events proved, the Lühring family's decision to move west to Kansas may well have saved Theodore Roeber's health and life, for he and his wife would follow her family to Washington County, Kansas in 1876. There, in the towns of Lanham and Hanover, the Lower-Saxony accents of the German settlers predominated. Many years later, after Theodore and Maria had moved to Colorado, stories continued to circulate that Maria paid each of her children a penny to speak only German in her presence. Her own accent apparently also amused her husband who was known to find her locutions peculiar—a reaction that will be thought deeply ironic by anyone familiar with the sometimes almost unintelligible accent of Saxon German in the Ore Mountains where the Roeber family had long lived, and which Theodore still spoke.

However, prior to relocating to Kansas and then Colorado, Theodore and Maria had settled down to the life of farming on the Roeber property in Lake County, Indiana. Within the first two years of their marriage, they suffered the loss of their first two children. Christian Gottlieb was born and died on October 12, 1869. His brother Theodore was born and died in November of 1870. Only on May 8, 1872, did a daughter, Maria Augusta, survive to become the first of 12 children, nine of whom would live into adulthood.

Perhaps still peeved regarding the disposition of his father's land, on May 21, 1870, in the Lake County Common Pleas Court, Theodore filed suit against his mother and two legitimate sisters asking for a re-partition of his father's property. Ultimately, he withdrew the cause against his mother, waived a jury trial, and was apparently content with the court finding in favor of his petition. That finding held that he and his two sisters were to be equal owners of the land to be held in fee simple (that is, total ownership of land and structures there-on) reserving Bertha's already-settled one-third of the original property as her right as Christian's widow.

Three months later, on August 8, 1870, Theodore and his wife Maria received a warranty deed in exchange for one dollar that ceded Hedwig Bertha (Roeber) Planer's property to her older brother. For the next six years, Theodore and Maria farmed both Theodore's and Hedwig Bertha's portions of Christian's original property while Bertha remained in the original home. Augusta took her portion of the property into her first marriage with Otto Steinbach. A surviving note in Steinbach's hand, dated Chicago, July 2, 1870, stipulated "I allowed with this, my brother-in-law to take the haye of the thventy *[twenty]* four acres of my land in North Township, In. and nobody else as this named brother-in-law Theodore Roeber is allowed to take it." A year after providing Theodore with this note, Otto and Augusta Steinbach became parents of a son, Louis Carl. Years later, a note from Louis thanked his uncle informing him "that we got the rabbits and they where just as good as you send them the first day but they are a little dry but that did not hurd *[hurt]*. And I tell you that I am in the third reader now and I will write you some more the next time." Moving to Chicago with his mother and her new husband Nicholas Schneider, Louis began life as a farmer but at age 35 he would be killed suddenly in a freak accident on May 23, 1906, when he was struck by lightning as he was watering his team of horses on his farm.

Theodore's sister Augusta Hedwig Roeber, having married Nicholas Schneider, rejoiced in 1875 at the survival of their first child, William, and that same year Augusta witnessed the baptism of her niece, Theodore Roeber's daughter Mary.

The Schneider family is referenced in the court testimony from the 1920s. At that time, Mary (married surname Mak), the youngest of the three children born out of wedlock to Bertha, recalled that as far as she knew, it was Franz Planer who rented the portion of land that had come to her sister Augusta Hedwig Schneider, and she recalled that Planer had always farmed it. As far as she knew, both the Planers and Schneiders had always claimed to own the land. Mary Mak testified that she had not known that "Hedwig sold hers to Theodore or traded with Theodore, and Theodore conveyed his land to Franz Planer." What she did recall was a conversation with Bertha who had complained to Mary Mak that "she couldn't talk English and they did just as they wanted with her." Franz Planer's son Frank S. Planer testified that Bertha's three youngest (illegitimate) children were regarded by the Planers as "stepbrother and sister," and his youngest sister Hattie (Planer) Parker recalled in her testimony that the youngest children's natural father had been a "hired hand of Germany"—whose name was rumored to be "Glazer." In one of the last letters which she wrote before her own death in 1979, Hattie Parker recalled that hers was a big family and was used to "rough farmer food not store candy and cakes, it was farm vegetables, eggs, fruit and our own beef and pork and egges, chickens, ducks & geese and when Mary Mak brought 'goodies' from her store we were in our Heavenly Glory."

The record of deeds for Lake County reveals that, on August 8, 1870, Frank Planer and his wife Hedwig Bertha gave a warranty deed to Theodore Roeber for the nominal sum of $1.00. Theodore and his wife Maria lived on their farm next to the Planers. Whatever long-range plans Theodore may have had for his property in Indiana, by 1872 he was ill. Remaining in the hot, humid summers and bitterly cold winters of northern Indiana at the base of Lake Michigan became an increasingly unattractive prospect.

On May 16, 1876, Theodore and Maria sold their property to Christian Hoker for the sum of $1,200 and on the same day, Hoker mortgaged the land back to Theodore. Hoker then signed an agreement with Theodore dated May 19th promising that "one year after date I promise to pay to the order of Theodor Roeber Twenty Eight Dolars withouth any interest Value received. Due Mai 19th 1877." This agreement lasted until May 24, 1881, when Theodore and Maria released the mortgage because Christian Hoker had sold the property to Christian Hodel, who then mortgaged the land back to Hoker. By the early 1880s, Theodore's interest in the Indiana property had come to an end. In March and April of 1881, he received a letter from Crown Point Indiana informing him that Christian Hoker had promised to "try and pay the whole claim, including the $406.00 note." His correspondent asked Theodore to send, by registered letter, the notes, mortgage and cancellation of the mortgage since "Hocker expects to get the money by the 20th inst, *[instant, that is, a recent occurrence in the current month]* & perhaps sooner. He wants you to throw off some, and he thinks you will &c If you can consistently throw off some, why it would help him wonderfully... Don't fail to attend to this matter at once, because if he looses the chance to borrow the money will have to foreclose the mortgage to get the money..." In April 1881, Theodore received a letter from Franz Planer informing him that Hoker intended to sell out and move to Hammond itself. While Theodore was receiving Hoker's monthly payments, he had been living with his in-laws in Hanover, Kansas, and it was not until 1882 that he would be able to secure a warranty deed for his own property in Kansas.

In the meantime, just as Hoker sold the original property and moved to Hammond, Theodore's mother Bertha also relocated there. Bertha had found a home with Oscar and Willie Heckelman, who both intended to find work in the State Line Slaughterhouse. The slaughterhouse had begun operation in 1869 and, by the 1880s, that industry's success had caused the town of Hammond to expand to over 5,000 people. Ironically, the presence in Hammond of skilled butchers—many of them German-speakers—did not include the Roeber family whose ancestors in the Saxon town of Zschopau had, for several centuries, been known for their eminence in this skilled guild.

Theodore's move from Indiana to Kansas occurred only four months after a daughter, Augusta Wilhelmina, had been born on February 16, 1876—the child had lived only four days. In traveling to Kansas, Theodore was accompanied by two surviving children, Maria Augusta who had been born in 1872, and Frank Leonard, born in 1874. Prior to leaving Indiana, Maria Augusta, had been baptized on Christmas Day 1875 by the Lutheran pastor Herman Wunderlich who was serving in neighboring Tolleston. She was three years old, and her aunt Augusta Hedwig (Roeber) Schneider was one of the two witnesses. One-year-old Frank Leonard was also baptized in Indiana before the family began its move west. Ultimately, the family arrived in Washington County, Kansas, in June of 1876.

The choice of Washington County, Kansas as a new home came about because of the 1858 arrival from Hanover, Germany, of Sophia Brockmeyer and Gerat Hollenberg. Settling in northeastern Kansas Territory, they built a home where the roads from St. Joseph and Independence, Missouri, met. By the late 1860s their settlement and store also served as the Hollenberg Station of the Pony Express. In the 1860s, settlers on their way further west could obtain a meal and lodging in one of the nine rooms of the Hollenberg Station for 27 cents. Only by the 1860s did this part of Kansas become an area open to European settlement. Previously, the Pawnee, the Kansa and Kaw, and the Otoe-(Jiwere)-Missouria hunted and lived in the region. Eventually, the tribes traded with European settlers who increasingly were German-speakers. Hollenberg himself began laying plans in 1869 for a town to bear the name Hanover—in honor of the kingdom into which he had been born.

The arrival of the St. Joseph & Denver City Railroad in 1870 tied Marysville, Kansas, to Hastings, Nebraska. This rail line increased the rate of in-migration by German-speakers who, until the First World War, spoke predominantly the dialect of Hanover and neighboring "low-German" regions of what would emerge in 1871 as Imperial Germany. That railroad crossed the tracks of the Burlington & Missouri River Railroad, a junction which would further connect Hollenberg's emerging town to larger settlements in Nebraska, Missouri, Iowa, and Illinois.

By 1870, both a German Evangelical Society and a Roman Catholic Church had been built in Hanover, followed by the founding of Zion Lutheran Church and a German-speaking Methodist Church in 1874. The St. Joseph & Denver City Railroad and the Catholic Church promoted settlement among German immigrants, promising large farming lands as well as business and housing lots. For those who chose to live in the town of Hanover itself, a *Turnverein* (a gymnastics and physical exercise club) and a brewery provided both employment and cultural advancement of German-speaking groups. It was into this growing community that Heinrich Lühring and his wife Katherine Maria had moved by the time Theodore and Maria had settled on the Indiana land which Theodore had inherited.

The controversy that broke out in the 1920s over the division of Christian Roeber's Indiana property revealed the great extent to which Theodore remained in closest family and business contact with certain individuals: his sister Hedwig Bertha and her husband, his childhood friend, Franz Planer in Indiana; and his in-laws, the Lühring family in Hanover, Kansas. He also received a number of letters (all in German) from his sister Augusta and her husband Nicholas Schneider in Chicago. In one surviving letter, written in

1887, Augusta pleaded with Theodore to reconsider his notion to move even farther West—especially because he was now a man with a family, and she believed her brother and his family would be better cared for in the company of relatives.

During this same period, Nicholas Schneider wrote a blunt letter to Theodore airing his negative views of developments in Indiana. Concerning Christian Heckelman, he wrote to say that Bertha's children felt that man took advantage of Bertha's naïve trust and belief in the Heckelman family, especially Willie Heckelman who, Schneider wrote, "is known in all of Hammond, yes, in all of Indiana as a lazy drunkard." But Schneider knew that some of his opinions would likely cause an uproar in the family at large and ended his letter to his "dear brother-in-law" thusly: "...say nothing to Mother or the others because you know how it will cause animosity."

Despite Theodore's and Schneider's initially poor opinion of both Christian and Willie Heckelman, more cordial relations later existed between Theodore and younger members of the Heckelman family. Theodore wrote from Hanover, in October of 1877: "Dear little Ida and Willi we are all well and hope you are the same and your little Cousins Mari and Frank ar Reading at home in the pictdorial primer." Ida, and later Anita and Edward Heckelman, would continue to remain in contact with the Roeber family of Colorado into the 1960s.

By the time Theodore and Maria moved with their two children to Hanover, Washington County, Kansas, the influx of immigrants and the growth of this predominantly German-speaking town had made land purchases far more expensive than they had been a mere six years earlier. Not only had Theodore and Maria lived with Heinrich Lühring as they looked for property they could afford. They also, three years after their arrival, signed a covenant by which Heinrich and Maria Lühring agreed to sell 160 acres of land ("The South West quarter of Section Eleven in Township Two South of Range Five East of 6th P.M.") for $480. A provision of the purchase was that, within three years at a ten percent interest rate, Theodore could meet the payments. If, however, by 1882 a warranty deed could be produced by Theodore, then the covenant obligation would be voided.

On April 16, 1881, Theodore and Maria obtained the warranty deed for the land for the sum of $800. Available land lay toward the settlement of Lanham, some eight miles northwest of Hanover, straddling the state line with Nebraska. When they signed the contract deed, the land on which Theodore and Maria settled did not include a house; they lived in a dugout on the property.

In the end, the property proved to be problematic. After his family's eventual move to Colorado in 1888, Theodore's in-laws (Heinrich and his son Wilhelm Lühring, who remained in Kansas) attempted to look after Theodore's property interests there. In a later attempt to sell the land, Theodore and Mary's relatives in Kansas reminded the Colorado settlers that finding a buyer for the Kansas property (land which the Lühring family themselves then rented and farmed) was proving to be a challenge. This was not only, as they explained to Theodore, because of the lack of an actual house on the land, but also because the quality of the soil was poor—being full of many rocks and sticky clay *(Gumboden).*

By April 1887, a decade after his arrival in Kansas, Theodore took out a promissory note to Wilhelm Schele, stipulating that: "Four months & half after date I promise to pay to the order of Wm Schele Twenty-two dollars at 6 percent per annum." In February of 1888, Theodore came to an agreement with Wilhelm Lühring in which the latter rented Theodore's property "for the sum of one Hundred and twenty-five dollars." The property was identified as "The SW quarter of Section Eleven From two Range five in Washington County Kansas. Rents become due as follows: Feb. 1st 1889 Feb 1 1890."

Finally, in June of 1891, Theodore and Maria entered into another covenant relationship with Heinrich Dürer for the sum of $4,600. Dürer managed to secure a warranty deed by July of the following year and Theodore and Maria finally sold their Kansas land for $2,300, but it is unlikely that they received the entire sum in one payment, as the previous patterns of covenant deeds, warranty deeds, and mortgage agreements in both Indiana and in Kansas seem to indicate.

Theodore's struggles to remain a man of some property, income, and standing can be traced through these land sales. His father had, in 1854, paid $159.75 for the swamp lands property in Indiana, from which Theodore managed—only over the course of many years—to secure $1,200 from the sale of his portion by 1881. He had re-invested $800 in the Kansas farm by 1879 and managed to sell it for $2,300 in 1892, but apparently not in a lump sum arrangement. Just how fortunate Theodore and Maria were to have sold the Kansas property by 1892 became clear a year later. The "Panic" of 1893 sent the value of land, agricultural products, mining interests, and manufacturing into an even worse recession than the United States had experienced in the bleak days of 1877.

Despite the sale of the land in Indiana in 1881, Theodore had concluded by the early 1880s that the property in Kansas would never turn a profit, nor was life in Kansas improving his health. Washington County, Kansas experiences hot, humid summers and very cold, dry winters with temperatures that can vary from a winter low of 3 degrees Fahrenheit to 101 degrees during the summers. Theodore's pursuit of a pension by the early 1880s also reflected the fragile condition of his health. He apparently began thinking of this in 1877 because he received in May of that year a copy of his honorable discharge papers, the original of which he had lost. The stipulation on the copy was that it had been issued upon the sworn testimony of the applicant and the certificate could not be used for "claims" against the United States, nor for pay, or bounty but was simply evidence of "honorable service rendered." The certificate was also made invalid by transfer.

Although northeastern Kansas may have proven slightly more conducive to improving his chronic asthma, by 1881 Theodore kept among his business papers a price list for "D. Langel's Asthma and Catarrh Remedy" available from Apple Creek, Wayne County, Ohio, or the Aster House in New York City. (Catarrh is a buildup of mucus in the nose, throat, and sinuses.) The medicines were supposed to be sold only to wholesale druggists and dealers in medicine, costing $8.00 pre-paid by mail for a dozen bottles to be sold at retail for $1.00 apiece. Theodore had also seen the advertisement and accompanying application form for "medicated washes" to treat "thousands of persons laboring under Consumption, Asthma, Bronchitis, Nasal Catarrh, Loss of Voice, etc." who Dr. N.B. Wolfe promised "have been restored to health by my method of inhaling remedies."

Theodore communicated by mail with Dr. Wolfe and this specialist in Cincinnati asked Theodore to describe medicines he had taken, tobacco smoked, chewed or taken as snuff; use of "spirituous liquors" and record of pulse beats per minute and whether he was "naturally of a joyous disposition." In the doctor's return letter, he concluded that "the disease is catarrh. The membrane lining the nose throat and bronchial tubes is its Seat. Its presence causes the secretions of unhealthy mucus. This means by reason of its morbid character will in[fect] the subjacent healthy parts within disease. In this way the disease will extend itself... There is now a tubercular deposit upon the lungs that will worsen and cause them to break down if proper remedies are not made to prevent. I believe the treatment would help you..."

In his leather pocketbook, along with his original baptismal certificate and other important papers, Theodore kept a list of ingredients (whether prescribed by Wolfe is uncertain) that included "carbonate of ammonia 2 drams, alum, 1 dram, capsiena, foreign gentian Colombe root and Prussiate of iron of each ½ dram, Virginia Snakeroot and valerian root, of each 2 drams." Below this mixture is a note to add "Sulphuric ether with aqua ammonia, of each 1 ounce, and, muriate of ammonia, 1/8 ounce."

From a series of letters complaining of continued lung trouble Theodore wrote to his son Gustave, one can deduce that none of these remedies proved useful. Those letters were written during Theodore's travels to warmer climates in an effort to escape Colorado winters, from around 1909 until his death in 1916.

Between 1876 and 1888, as Theodore struggled to make the Kansas land profitable, he and Maria Dorothea expanded their family with the arrival of Elizabeth Dorothea in April of 1877, Clara Elizabeth in March 1879, Gustave Wilhelm in February 1881, Adolph Christian in February 1883, Margaretha Catharina in March 1885, and Ludwig Heinrich in April 1887. Unlike the couple's sad experience in suffering the deaths of their first three children in Indiana, all of these later children lived into adulthood. By 1883, Zion Evangelical Lutheran Church had been built in Hanover, and both baptismal and confirmation certificates survive for at least some of these children.

The attempt to make the Kansas farm profitable included investment in at least some equipment. Theodore looked to Chicago for the most part as the source of both equipment and seeds for planting crops, flowers, and trees. His interest in a McCormick Reaper and Mower led him to retain the business card of J.H. Prier at Crown Point, Indiana, for information on the cost of the machine. Henry Weber's Wagon firm on West Lake Street in Chicago informed Theodore that it would be cheaper for him to buy from the firm's Kansas City agents, the Weir Plough Company for $70.00. Thorn Wire Hedge Company on Madison Street in Chicago supplied Theodore with descriptions of their barbed wire fencing. But so did The Chicago Galvanized Wire Fence Company at No. 9 Wabash Avenue, which touted their patented twisted galvanized two-wire and zinc-coated fencing "completely soldered together from end to end." L.M. Ramsey & Co. on North Main Street in St. Louis, Missouri, a branch of the Seneca Falls Pump and Fire Engine Works, gave Theodore a price list for a well pump that included fitting the pipe and connecting it to the pump, for a total cost of $25.95. J.C. Vaughan in Chicago gave Theodore a price list for bulbs, seeds, and trees, informing him that they had just received an order from his mother, Bertha Heckelman. Theodore's 1876 order for seeds cost an initial $1.50 for 10 papers of seeds. However, Vaughan noted that "the package of Leek and the flower seeds have not yet arrived, but I will send them as soon as they come. I sent you a paper which gives you the market price of timothy and clover seeds here." He offered to send a short list of seeds in German and then asked Theodore if he wanted new seeds or last year's seeds at half price. The latter included cabbages, tomatoes, carrots, onions, Bohnen *[beans]*, Rote Beeten *[red beets]*, Melons, "and so forth." The personal connection to Vaughan became clear at the end of his list: "I have not been to Dolton lately so I can't give you much news," indicating the town in Illinois outside Chicago where Theodore and Maria had been married in 1868.

Vaughan explained that in addition to sending seeds for crops he could also supply dahlias, but it was too early to set them out. Likewise, if the Roeber family wanted to plant trees, Vaughn could supply "young evergreens 1 ft high for 10c each if you take 50 trees. I have some nice 1 year old grape vines for 5c each."

Since no surviving photographs exist of either the interior of the Kansas dugout nor of its surrounding lands, we can only speculate about what was planted, what survived, and how these prices suggest whether Theodore and his expanding family were improving their material well-being or threatened with possible ruin. That he at least attempted to plant trees is evident from a receipt from the "Timber-Culture Receiver's Office" sent on September 10, 1879, from the U.S. Land Office in Kirwin, Kansas. That receipt acknowledged his $14.00 payment on the "NW ¼ of Section 21 in Township 3 of Range 36 under the act of Congress approved June 14, 1878 entitled, 'An Act to amend an act entitled 'An Act to encourage the growth of timber on the Western Prairies.'"

(The original "Timber Culture Act of 1873" was one of several congressional acts passed to encourage western settlement, ironically undercut by other acts, especially the Desert Land Act of 1877 that was exploited by unscrupulous speculating companies who paid scant attention to what de-forestation on the fragile western prairies would unleash—a bitter lesson learned by the farming communities of the "Dust Bowl" in the 1930s.)

In 1880, Theodore received a letter from a friend, Charles Hoeland, then living in Topeka, Kansas. Hoeland recited a grim story of having planted wheat and sorghum on his farm (whose location he did not identify) only to have a hot windstorm destroy all of the crops. Most of the settlers in his former neighborhood he wrote, had by now left, or were seeking work on the railroad. In Topeka itself an Aid Committee had been founded "that does more for the western sufferers as the Government." Hoeland had found work as a stone mason and could earn $2.25 to $2.50 per day, and he was renting three rooms for $10.00 that he described as a bargain since the rents in Topeka were very high.

Historians have documented in detail the global nature of a "long recession" that began with the Panic of 1873 and only started to improve by late 1879. Repeated recessions succeeded that initial period of crisis with stagnation in wages through the late 1880s. For the farmers and townspeople of Washington County this downturn included the bankruptcy of the St. Joseph & Denver City Railroad in 1884, a collapse that slowly improved when the Union Pacific absorbed the line in 1888.

For residents of the American Midwest, droughts also contributed to the miseries of agricultural communities, laying the groundwork for the rise of the Populist Party in the 1890s. No surviving evidence suggests that Theodore Roeber was ever tempted to question his allegiance to the party of Abraham Lincoln. While in Kansas, he used an attorney who was a member of the Republican Executive Committee in Lake County, Indiana to complete the sale of his property to Christian Hoker. He also sought out connections to the local Republican Party in Kansas; served on the school board for his rural region of the county; and by 1883 served as Adjutant for the Grand Army of the Republic's Johnson Post No. 21. He made sure that he was transferred officially to the GAR's Kansas Post Number 5 at Kearney, Nebraska, by May 1888 in order not to lose the $4.00 per month pension he had been granted, and whose amount he would later ask to be increased. By May of 1897 he had been appointed "Inspector" for Post #86 for the GAR Department of Colorado & Wyoming headquartered at Denver.

The memories of the Kansas farm passed on by Theodore's children and a lone photograph give a slightly more detailed picture of life on this prairie in the 1870s and 80s. At some point during the late 1870s, a professional photographer captured Theodore, Maria, and their two oldest surviving children seated in a formal dress and pose. The ages of their children can only be guessed at, but both young Mary and Frank appear to be between four to six years of age. At that time, Theodore was still clean-shaven and appears much as he does in the photograph with Frank Planer taken at the age of 19. In that earlier image, Planer sported the goatee which he wore for the balance of his life. This photograph must have hung on the wall of the Kansas dugout, along with the framed copy of his GAR honorable discharge papers. Theodore did not hang a copy of the photograph of his mother, Bertha, which can be seen adorning the wall of the Planer home in Indiana when Theodore and Maria were visiting in the mid-1890s.

Upon reaching Kansas, Theodore and Maria's eldest daughter Mary, along with her younger siblings, were able to attend a basic grammar school that had been built a mile away from the farm. In young Mary's case, while going to school, she lived with her relative, Elizabeth Lühring-Weyer. Apparently, that connection proved important because Theodore's grand-daughter, Dorothy Sellars, later recalled that her mother Mary, at some point, went to live with "Lizzie" because she was not getting along with her father. Sellars concluded her recollection of her mother's memory by observing, "I don't think my grandfather was a very nice man."

Mary Roeber's younger sister, Elizabeth Dorothea, helped to keep watch over the few cattle that grazed on the prairie. The children did this in groups of two or three and, while herding with her younger brother Gustave, Elizabeth was gored by one of the bulls, resulting in a life-long scar. Adolph (Otto) Christian, born in 1883, was too young to participate in the herding of the cattle but was given the task by his mother of taking food and water to the older children. On one such day, a thunder and lightning storm broke over the prairie, setting the grass on fire while Otto was delivering lunch. The boy alerted his mother who called all the children to take up burlap sacks, soak them in the creek that flowed near the house, and use the wet sacks to beat out the flames.

In another incident, in 1888, just as the family was preparing to leave for Colorado, five-year old Otto climbed onto the seat of the farm wagon and released the brake. Years later, his older brother Gus recalled that the wagon and child had rolled down the knoll on which the wagon was kept and was stopped only when the tongue of the wagon plowed a furrow that ended in the creek which flowed into the Little Blue River nearby. When the time came for the trip to Colorado, Otto was excited since he had watched trains on the St. Joseph & Denver City Railroad route pass near the farm again in 1888—that busy rail line having become a part of the Union Pacific.

The only other descriptions of the Kansas farm appear in a sole-surviving letter written in German by Maria Dorothea to her absent husband Theodore. Although the year is uncertain, it was probably written in 1887. Her letter of 10 July to her "Dear Husband," noted that his letter had arrived, and she hoped that his Fourth of July had been more enjoyable than theirs.

She and her daughter Mary had spent the entire day planting corn and then she had accompanied the child to celebrations (perhaps in Hanover) since she was not willing to have Mary attend alone because of the dangers of firecrackers. She hoped he would be home by the 19th because she had far too much to do, weeds were growing so high that crops were hard to see, including her sugar-corn although the wheat crop was still doing reasonably well. "The children ask every day when their papa is coming home again and when I answer he is not coming yet then they say, Oh, we also aren't allowed to leave—but lately they have not asked as often."

The memories passed down by Theodore's children include their father's decision to take his thirteen-year-old son Frank with him and leave the balance of the family in the Spring of 1887 for a trip west to Colorado. His son Ludwig Heinrich was born on April 4, 1887, and one assumes that Theodore waited to see the safe birth of his youngest son before bringing Frank with him on the long journey west, taking advantage of more clement spring and summer weather for travel. Assuming that the memories are correct, Theodore and Frank travelled by buckboard drawn by mules as far as Colorado Springs. Their subsequent journey remains wrapped in mystery and conjecture.

According to the memories Theodore's granddaughters put into their typescript in the 1960s, Theodore and Frank went first to the mining town of Rico. Then, to escape the bitter winter in Rico, they journeyed in late autumn to Durango, Colorado. This is almost certainly a confused and false memory. The more likely journey would have taken the two south out of Colorado Springs past Pueblo, and from there to Walsenburg. The only way west from this point would have been to Alamosa. Following the Rio Grande River through Monte Vista, they would have struck a trail over the Continental Divide—a route first established generations earlier by the First Peoples of Colorado known as the Utes. Since a road over Wolf Creek Pass to Pagosa Springs did not exist until 1916, the trail had to have been the one which went over Elwood Pass. (This was the route critics argued for in the early 20th century instead of the more daunting challenges of the Wolf Creek approach. The Elwood Pass even today joins U.S. 160 some miles further south of Wolf Creek Pass, eventually reaching Durango.)

What attracted Theodore to Durango also remains a matter of conjecture. By the time he and his son arrived, this town was already active as a smelting center for the rich veins of silver ore that were being mined in the San Juan Mountains to the north. The air quality would not have been such that someone suffering from respiratory difficulties would have chosen to settle there. It may well have been this discovery that led them on their subsequent journey north on the road that had only just been completed by the redoubtable Otto Mears (1840–1931). Mears had established a toll road from Durango north to Ridgway but, in constructing this route along the east branch of the Dolores River, Mears planned from the beginning to turn the road into what became the Rio Grande & Southern Railroad. By 1891 he had succeeded in connecting Durango to the headquarters of his railroad in Ridgway. The route included the towns of Dolores, Rico, and Placerville, over Lizard Head Pass. By arriving at Ridgway, Theodore and Frank would have then turned further north an additional 26 miles to Montrose, their final destination.

No surviving documents suggest that Theodore ever met his contemporary Mears. But they had much in common. The latter, like Theodore had arrived alone as a minor in the United States; both were Civil War Union veterans—Mears serving in the First California Infantry Regiment, Theodore in the Ninth Illinois Volunteer Cavalry. Moreover, both settled in Colorado only after previous attempts at establishing themselves financially in other areas of the country. But their histories diverged sharply as well. Mears had tried his hand at several different occupations whereas Theodore had grown up knowing only a life on a farm. And Mears, by the late 1880s was already a wealthy man who was fluent in several languages, including that of the Utes. Theodore, while aspiring to wealth and status, never came close to the standard of living which Mears enjoyed nor to complete fluency in English. Theodore would end his life in Colorado some years after Mears' 1893 financial collapse. That misfortune led Mears to leave Colorado, engage in further business ventures in the eastern United States, and eventually to die in Pasadena, California.

Arriving in Montrose, Theodore decided on renting a farm in Oak Grove near Montrose. But why this location was chosen also remains unclear. The Los Pintos Agency of the U.S. government had in 1875 moved to the Uncompahgre Valley and by 1880 a military garrison had been located four miles north of the Agency. With the removal of most of the Utes from Colorado that same year, the settlement that became Montrose began to take shape. Nonetheless, there was nothing in the composition of the early town that suggested a German-speaking presence, nor is it clear how news of the removal of the Utes and the opening up of this part of Colorado to settlers would have reached the Roeber family in Washington County, Kansas.

By whatever means Theodore learned of the Montrose area, he and his son completed their journey and then began the long trip back to Kansas, although their return route remains unknown. The distance between Hanover, Kansas, and Colorado Springs (459.6 miles) entails, in the twenty-first century, a seven hour and 18-minute drive by automobile at Interstate speeds. A trip by mule-drawn buckboard, assuming favorable weather and approximately 30 miles per day, would have taken 19 days, i.e. the better part of three weeks. The journey from Durango to Montrose would, again, have taken at least two or more weeks, depending on weather.

The entire area of western Colorado had been opened to extensive settlement with the Treaty of 1880 that had been negotiated with the Ute Indian Nation led by Chief Ouray who himself died in 1880. A heavily disputed interpretation of that treaty resulted in the removal to a reservation in Utah of the Uncompahgre Agency Utes of which Ouray (a member of the Tabeguache clan; one of the seven Ute bands) had been the leading Chief. The actual provision of the Treaty envisioned the Utes settling on agricultural lands near the present town of Grand Junction, Colorado. The removal of the Utes who had been part of the Uncompahgre Agency meant that lands near Ouray's former residence at Colona, and the eventual neighboring town of Montrose, were now open to settlement by non-Indians.

Founded formally in 1882, Montrose offered a better climate for Theodore's asthmatic condition as well as agricultural lands for newcomers. Once again, one of Otto Mears' enterprises indirectly influenced Theodore's decisions because, in 1881, William Palmer's Denver & Rio Grande Railroad had purchased Mears' Toll Road over Marshall Pass—reaching Gunnison on the Western Slope in 1881 and completing a line through the Black Canyon of the Gunnison to reach Montrose in September 1882. Theodore would have learned when he and Frank arrived, that he could move his family and goods by narrow gauge railroad from Salida on the eastern side of the Continental Divide where the standard gauge rails ended, to the fledgling western slope settlements. Whether Theodore and Frank returned to Kansas by train, using the Marshall Pass route through the Continental Divide, also remains a matter of speculation.

The farm Theodore rented, however, was located either in Oak Grove, or Maple Grove, settlements just to the west of the town of Montrose itself. The move to Colorado did not take place upon the sale of the Kansas property. Somehow, Theodore must have managed to obtain a sufficient amount of cash to sell his livestock and put household furnishings and at least a wagon on a railroad freight car. He and Frank, according to family memory came in an "emigrant car" while the rest of his family boarded a standard-gauge passenger coach (the particular line is not known) for the trip to Colorado that ended in Salida. Which line the remaining Roeber family took to leave Kansas for Colorado is also unclear. They could have loaded both freight and themselves at Hanover, using the old St. Joseph & Denver City line now belonging to the Union Pacific, and travelled northwest through Nebraska, where they may have left the mainline that continues through Wyoming to Salt Lake City to connect to a southwesterly line into Denver. They would have had to change to the Denver & Rio Grande Railroad in that city for the journey south through Colorado Springs, then Pueblo, and through the "Royal Gorge" route to Salida before changing to the narrow-gauge line over Marshall Pass, passing through Gunnison and part of the Black Canyon to eventually reach Montrose.

Rather than the foregoing, the more likely route to Colorado would have been one that took them south from Hanover through Marysville with an eventual connection to the Atchison, Topeka, & Santa Fe line that ran west through La Junta, Colorado, and then to Pueblo. In Pueblo, they would have had to change to the D&RG and then north to the town of Salida and the narrow-gauge line over the Rocky Mountains. This so-called "Scenic Line of the World" follows the Gunnison River through the Black Canyon of the Gunnison and past the famous Curecanti Needle before leaving the canyon at Cimmaron, then reaching Cerro Summit and finally, Montrose. So close to the riverbed were the tracks and the constant danger of falling rock so real that train crews dreaded this route. The world-travelled British writer and explorer Rudyard Kipling admitted admiring the spectacular scenery but being terrified of the possibility of imminent catastrophe. The railroad eventually extended its line to Delta and Grand Junction by 1883, but it would be another 20 years before the Roeber family could again make use of rail transportation since they stayed in the Oak Grove area for only a year, arriving sometime in 1888 before moving further into mountainous country where the Denver & Rio Grande would not reach until the early twentieth century.

On February 28, 1889, Theodore and Maria's last child to reach adulthood (Augusta Juliana) was born at the Oak Grove property. When she was but three weeks old, the family moved a final time in March to the property Theodore had discovered while on a hunting trip. This time, perhaps at his wife's pleading, he had found a predominantly German-speaking rural community in rolling foothills at the base of the West Elk Mountains, the westernmost extension of the Rockies, and in a high desert climate that finally promised to bring both improved health, and the possibility of a profitable farming enterprise. His children Frank, Mary, Clara, Elizabeth and "Augustus" appear on a surviving roster of students for Maple Grove school near the rented property somewhere between Oak Grove and Maple Grove. (*Augustus*, in fact Gustave, was not named for a Roman Emperor or a Christian bishop; the name means "glorious guest," or "staff of the gods.") By March of 1889 the family had rented a portion of the land in the North Fork Valley of the Gunnison River that had been homesteaded earlier in 1883.

Theodore's earlier activities in Kansas had begun to reveal a pattern of behavior and self-presentation that he developed even further in Colorado. While in Kansas, he had involved himself in local school affairs, serving as a clerk to the local school district. In the course of his duties, he became entangled in a dispute over the purchase of a set of maps. The surviving correspondence reveals a first draft of a letter he made before sending the fair copy, revealing a good, but accent-influenced command of the English language, a penmanship that guaranteed legibility in his record-keeping, and an insistence on a respect for his reputation for honesty and trustworthiness.

In his letter of October 16, 1883, to H.C. Robinson, the Superintendent of Schools for Washington County, Kansas, Theodore reviewed the reasons for the controversy. He reminded Robinson that "the School board is authorized to buy only 1 map in place of a set. I addressed a postal card to your address some time ago but received no answer ub *[up]* to this time. I did write to you because I had met the District treasurer some time ago and we talked about the map in question. Finly *[Finally]* we agreed that I should write to you and see what you would say abound *[about]* it. So, I did write the Postal Cart *[Card]* next day comes School director to my Hand and wants an order for the maps. I then told him that I had written a Postal Card to see what you would say about it. As per agreement with the District treasurer (his father) thence sais *[says]* he we will wait then until we get an answer. A few days later I met the Director again, Said he to me did you get an answer from the Superintendent." Contrary to his expectations, Theodore discovered that the maps had been ordered without his knowledge. He then concluded, "So Now dear Sir with this I tenter *[tender]* my resignation and am ready to pay me fine if there is any for I would never issue an order for those maps unless I got the authorization from the majority of the voters of the District because the proceeding called only for one map and not for a set. And I have found no body that would agree to bay *[pay]* $32.00 for those maps only but the district treasurer and director of course they are father and son they are both at one you may say they are the *[illegible]* would make a good director and I think you would be a good clerk for this district. . .I consider my self honest and always have been and have served to my country faithfully in arms and am still servand *[serving]* for my Comrades. Yours, Theodore Roeber."

On August 20, 1883, Theodore sent a similar letter while acting as adjutant to Johnson Post No. 21 of the GAR (Grand Army of the Republic) veterans. This letter was addressed to the Adjutant General Diefendorf expressing his concern that a possible communication to the post had been received but that the letter had not come from the Adjutant. "I think the same being written by some one that is not a member of the G.A.R." And again, he was concerned lest his own reputation for honesty be called into question.

Although Theodore involved himself in the affairs of the GAR and the local schools in Kansas, he does not appear to have been active in the one other institution that would naturally have appealed to immigrant German-speakers. Although Theodore and Maria were married by a Lutheran pastor in Indiana, and took pains to have their children baptized, the surviving German-language Lutheran churches in Washington county do not reveal Theodore and his wife as members. Maria's family, the Lührings, by contrast, do appear in those records and obituaries for Maria's parents suggest that they were active in the church. Since fire has destroyed some of the nineteenth-century church records, we cannot be certain that Theodore and Maria did not attend services during their time in Washington County. But a similar pattern would emerge once they settled in the North Fork of the Gunnison River Valley in Colorado. Itinerant German-speaking pastors of the Evangelical Lutheran Church of Missouri and Other States (today's Lutheran Church-Missouri Synod) did pass through the North Fork Valley from time to time. Often services were held at the Stewart Mesa Schoolhouse, an area just west of "German Mesa" and not far from the Roeber property. While Theodore's oldest daughter, Mary, attended those services, and later attended the Christian church in Paonia, no surviving evidence suggests that Theodore devoted any time to church matters. (Although, upon his death in 1916, the Lutheran Pastor Wegener did preside at the funeral at the Christian Church in the town some four miles north of the Roeber home.)

Within a few years of his arrival in western Colorado, Theodore devoted all of his time to expanding his initial land holding. He also participated in the formation and promotion of various ditch companies established to provide irrigation water for the high desert farms in the North Fork Valley. By 1895, he would also successfully run for office as County Assessor. Despite the apparent success of the move to Colorado—success which would inspire a local newspaper to take notice in 1899 of Theodore's prominence—his family life would be, by the mid-1890s, marked by tragedy and disappointment.

Sources

Indiana Property Files.

Powell A. Moore, *The Calumet Region: Indiana's Last Frontier* (n.p.: Indiana Historical Bureau, 1959).

Birth, Death, Marriage certificates, Lake County, Indiana.

Christian Roeber's Inventory of Estate (Lake County records, copies).

Federal Census for Lake County, Indiana, 1860, 1870.

Record of Suits brought in Common Pleas Court Lake County, Indiana, 1865-1870.

E.A. Davenport, ed., *History of the Ninth Regiment Illinois Cavalry Volunteers* (Chicago, 1888), 171-77; 263, 266.

Veterans' Pension application and supporting letters, 1876-1915.

Lühring Family File.

Theodore and Maria Roeber Picture Album.

Washington County Kansas Records File.

Delta County Records of Deeds.

Mamie Ferrier and George Sibley, *Long Horns and Short Tales: A History of the Crawford Country Vol I.* (1992), pp. 93-94.

Images of America: Montrose (Montrose County Historical Society & Museum, 2017), pp. 27, 78.

Don Koch, *The Colorado Pass Book,* 3rd ed. (Boulder, CO, 2000).

4x4explore.com

Wikipedia entry: "Otto Mears."

DRGW.Net "History."

1700s: An unknown artist's conception of the view of Zschopau, Saxony, Germany—the Roeber family's ancestral town as it would have appeared after the 1750 fire and subsequent rebuilding. (Undocumented engraving from the author's collection.)

1865 February: Theodore Roeber (left) and Franz Planer on the occasion of their enlistment in the 9th Illinois Volunteer Cavalry.

1876: Maria and Theodore Roeber with children Mary and Frank.

Theodore Roeber's mother Bertha (née Ulrich) and last name Heckleman by later second marriage.

1880s: The original house on the Roeber ranch.

1912: The second house on the Roeber ranch with brothers (left to right) Gus, Otto, Frank, and Louis Roeber.

Ca. 1913: Louis Roeber on the "dump-rake."

Ca. 1918: Louis H. Roeber

The 1928 Dodge with (left to right) Gus, Clinton, Arline, and Charlotte Roeber along with Grandmother Mary Caroline Alderson.

Ca. 1930: Fannie Roeber on horseback.

1934: (left to right) Charlotte Roeber, Dorothy Sellars, Arline Roeber, and Mary née Roeber Brown.

1938: Clinton Roeber's Paonia High School graduation photo.

Early 1950s: The author's father, Clinton Roeber, at a campfire.

1949: The author and his parents Clinton and Dorothy (née Trebeck) Roeber.

Remembering Reputation and Prosperity

1989: Four generations of the Roeber family on the occasion of the ranch's centennial celebration. Seated left to right: Julia Trebeck, Maria Roeber, Krissey Kossler holding Ian Roeber, Patricia Roeber holding Chase Roeber, Kelsey Kossler, Grete Roeber, and Jessica Roeber. Standing in second row: Dorothy (Trebeck) Roeber, Jenni Roeber, John Kossler and Jody Roeber. Standing in back row: Clinton Roeber, the author, Chad Roeber, Pat Roeber holding Christian Roeber, Denise Kossler, Steve Kossler, and Mark Roeber.

1995 family photo on the occasion of Clinton and Dorothy Roeber's 50th wedding anniversary. Front seated on ground are Chase and Ian Roeber. Seated, left to right: Patricia Roeber, Mark Roeber holding Anthony Roeber, Christian Roeber, Clinton and Dorothy Roeber, Denise Kossler, and (standing) Kelsey Kossler and Becca Roeber. Back row, left to right: Jessica Roeber, Jody Roeber, Grete Roeber, Maria Roeber, Pat Roeber, the author, John Kossler, Steve Kossler, Krissey Kossler, Jenni Roeber, and Chad Roeber.

Chapter Three
Fruit Growers, Cattlemen, Miners and Aliens

In August 1899, readers of a special edition of *The North Fork Times* newspaper published in Hotchkiss, Colorado, were alerted to the possibilities offered by one of the mesas surrounding the small town of Paonia, Colorado:

"German Mesa: This tract of land lies south and east of Paonia, and includes about 1,500 acres of tillable land, 800 acres of which is under cultivation. As the name would indicate, much thrift and many comfortable homes will be found here. The land is level and most of the ranches are along the German Creek, which traverses the mesa. It was first settled twelve years ago by Messrs. Myers and Eubanks. They are no longer residents of the Mesa. Among those who reside there at the present time are ex-county Assessor Roeber, Fred Lucas, J.L. Martin, M.P. Gonner, W.W. Wilcox, Peter Vogel, W.R. Crook, Levi Miller, John Lane, Malvin Lane, W.D. Wilcox, B.M. Ballard, F.A.E. Kline, Fred Koehne, Joseph Fluallen... Mr. Roeber has 520 acres, all under fence. He has 150 head of cattle, nice orchards and like thousands of other German Americans, has made for himself and his family an excellent home, and his orchard is one of the most promising in the North Fork Country."

The newspaper's attempt to encourage settlement on a mesa (that is not flat) and whose steadily increasing topography ended at the base of the 11,402-foot high Mount Lamborn had been home to Theodore Roeber and his family for a decade when the foregoing article appeared. Oral history among his children claimed that Theodore had discovered this area at the base of the West Elk Mountain range on a hunting trip, presumably in the Fall of 1888, not long after the family had settled in Oak Grove, near Montrose on their rented property. But it is also more than likely that his wife Maria, who never mastered the English language and paid her children not to speak English in her presence, may have influenced her husband to seek out a German-speaking settlement that would have been more to her liking and reminiscent of the communities she had known in Indiana and Kansas.

Theodore's property in the North Fork Valley described in the 1899 newspaper article was once supposed, according to oral history, to have included part of the homestead acreage belonging to Anton Bernard Orth. Orth had come to the region for the first time as part of a freight team organized from Lake City after the first explorations of the valley had been conducted by Samuel Wade, Enos T. Hotchkiss, and John McIntire in August of 1881. Orth, who came originally from Vienna, Austria, had been born in 1849. Anton Bernard had met Amelia Frederika Koehne in Lake City, Colorado. Amelia had been born in 1850 in Baden-Baden, and theirs was a mixed marriage, he Lutheran, she Roman Catholic. They married in 1882, and were parents of 13 children, of whom three died in infancy. Orth had worked as a hod carrier in Gunnison, the town that was at that time the county seat before the creation of Delta County. In Gunnison, he helped build the Levita Hotel before moving to the North Fork of the Gunnison River Valley. Orth did own property on German Mesa and would later sell to other German-speakers such as Peter Vogel—but he did not sell to Theodore and Maria Roeber.

In 1886, another pioneering couple, Frederick and Augusta Lukas, homesteaded a property that eventually became Section 16/14/91. A year later, part of Section 17 was added to this initial property. On the extreme southern edge of Section 16, the Lukas family either built (or had Anton Orth build *for them*) the house into which the Roeber family eventually moved. It became a two-room structure made of adobe and straw bricks. The house had seven-foot-high walls which were 18 inches thick, all plastered in the interior; the rafters and sheeting made of pine wood had been milled in Durango with cedar shingles covering the roof. Access to the second story was made from an outside ladder. When Theodore's son Gustave and grandson Clinton dismantled the house in the 1950s, they discovered the footprints of small children in the adobe, surviving evidence that the Lukas or Orth family had put the adobe and straw mixture into wooden forms which their children tramped to make the adobe bricks.

The actual history of this property became buried beneath an oral history which included descendants of the Orth family. As late as 1979, in an interview conducted with Orth's granddaughter, Betty Gannon, the Orth-Roeber connection was still being passed on as history. What is of more help in understanding the original house was the memory of a Mrs. Anna Straub, a neighbor of the Lukas family who remembered that the Creek—named for Lukas, flowed down a gully close enough to the house and spring runoffs occasionally flooded the interior floor, which—perhaps for this reason—remained a dirt floor.

In 1888, Orth had sold to Peter Vogel part of his properties on German Mesa. The aforementioned 1899 special edition newspaper article that lauded the virtues of German Mesa also noted that "Mr. Voegel has thirty acres in orchard; receives water from the Minnesota and has an abundance of it and has a beautiful house, large vineyard, wine cellar and various other conveniences which go to make the happiness of home life." The surviving plats of land records show that Orth's property lay some miles further to the north and west from the lands where Theodore and Maria had settled.

What Theodore and Maria did in acquiring property on German Mesa repeated the pattern already rehearsed in Indiana, and subsequently, in Kansas. On February 26, 1889, a bond for deed in the amount of $200 for 40 acres was signed by Theodore and Augusta and Frederick Lukas. The Roeber family moved in March, and the bond for deed was recorded in June of that same year. Eleven months later, on May 5, 1890, Theodore penciled this note in a surviving notebook: "Trouble with Lukas." But on the following day wrote: "Trouble settled with Lukas." A year and a half later, on December 1, 1891, the original bond was cancelled and a warranty deed for the first property recorded. On the same day, Theodore took out a mortgage deed to Lukas for both sections 16 and 17. Theodore would patent 160 acres in 1892. His daughter, Mary, also filed for 160 acres but her property would, by 1909, be divided between her brother Frank who purchased 40 acres, her brother Gus who bought another 40, and her brother-in-law Charles Wiening who purchased the remaining 80. By 1905, patents for 160 acres each can be identified for Gus and Otto Roeber.

By 1892, Theodore had acquired a parcel of land from M.P. Gonner. Located in Section 5, this parcel was not contiguous to Theodore's farm, and it was much closer to the town of Paonia in a spot where German Mesa descended into the area known as "Dry Gulch." This property needed irrigation water and Theodore's ownership of this parcel, which his son-in-law Charles Wiening worked on, explains why Theodore became the president of the Turner Ditch Company. This project took water from Minnesota Creek and passed through various farms on German Mesa, including the parcel Theodore had acquired. Later he sold the parcel, perhaps because if lay isolated from his main holdings further to the south.

At the time a 1905 retrospective on the North Fork Valley was published, Bernard Orth was pictured next to his two-story home half-way between Paonia and Hotchkiss on a farm of 30 acres "of extremely productive land, ten acres being in orchard. 'Barney,' as he is commonly known, is considered one of the best brick layers and plasterers in the valley" including work on Paonia's Bross Hotel "now in course of construction." Orth was hailed as "a master mechanic and artist in his line of work."

The purchase price which Theodore paid for the family's original 40 acres included the all-important "two- and one-half shares of stock in our certain irrigating ditch known as the Inter-ocean ditch taking water from the west branch of Minnesota creek." This purchase set the pattern for the subsequent expansion of the farm and the critically important issue of water rights, without which most of the lands higher than the river valley itself, could not sustain crops nor support a European-style human settlement. Property was purchased gradually through the bond for deed and warranty process, and only very little land the Roeber family acquired was ever "homesteaded."

A number of legislative acts encouraging settlement on western lands had begun even before the Civil War, including the act that had enabled Christian Roeber to buy swamp lands on the Indiana-Illinois border. Eventually, a variety of congressional acts would settle 1.6 million homesteaders on 160 million acres of land, nearly all of which were situated west of the Mississippi River. The Timber Culture Act of 1873 that had caught Theodore's attention in Kansas was followed, in 1877, by the Desert Land Act which, unlike previous homestead laws, did not require a person making a claim to be resident on the land. Amended in 1891, this act reduced the former requirement to pay 25 cents per acre on 640 acres of desert land, show proof of reclamation for three years and then upon proof to pay a balance of $1.00 per acre. The 1891 revision reduced the acreage to 320 and demanded that a map be shown of the proposed land with an irrigation plan. Improvements were to be made at the rate of $3.00 per acre with an additional $1.00 per acre that demonstrated how water was going to be used to reclaim desert land for cultivation. In 1894, the Carey Act allowed private companies to begin creating irrigation systems that they could then profit from by sale of water.

Various western states benefited from these acts that encouraged settlement on arid lands. By 1909, the Enlarged Homestead Act was passed. This act allowed 320 acres in lands not easily irrigated to be developed for dryland farming. In 1912, a Three-Year Homestead Act reduced to three years the time for a final application of a patent on homestead lands, replacing the more generous term of five years that had formerly been the case. Finally, in 1916, the Stockraising Homestead Act allowed 640 acres to be settled for the purpose of ranching, not farming. From the original rental and purchases Theodore had managed, he steadily increased his holdings. Beginning in 1889, he acquired 520 acres by the turn of the twentieth century, followed by a patent for 160 acres in 1895, and another by his daughter Mary in 1899.

(A land patent is obtained through a series of legal and public notice procedures allowing the patent-seeker to obtain right, title, and interest to a specifically defined area.)

The Roeber family's property holdings had steadily advanced since their arrival. Their initial trip from the Montrose area to the North Fork of the

Gunnison River Valley had required them to pass along the ironically named *Peach Valley Road*. The road took them through desolate adobe bluffs spanning two days with Maria and the youngest children aboard a wagon containing household possessions and a coop holding chickens and two peacocks. Milk cows were tied behind the wagon and the two eldest sons, Frank and Gustave, rode on horseback behind the cows. They forded the Gunnison River near the end of the Gunnison Gorge close to Horse Shoe Bend and it was here that the family made their overnight camp. Theodore's children recalled later that their father's rather droll sense of humor included offering them, as they grew thirsty during the second day of the trip, a ladle full of water to quench their thirst—only to discover that he had taken the water from a nearby mineral spring and was amused at the long faces that resulted from sampling the salty-tasting water.

During the first years on German Mesa, the children helped their parents clear additional purchased acres, dislodging the juniper trees, sagebrush and granite stones that had to be removed before any plantings or harvesting could be undertaken. Between 1889 and at least 1899, grain harvested on the farm had to be taken by horse-drawn wagon back to Montrose for grinding, a two-day trip each way. The Montrose Flour Mill had started in 1886 under the ownership of McCall and Clark. Located just north of the old, wooden railroad depot in Montrose, this mill had no rivals until in 1899 another mill was opened in Delta. Even later, in the early 1900s, a cooperative flour mill opened in Crawford, operated by water that flowed from the Clipper Ditch. Whether the Roeber family chose to use the Crawford Mill or made the longer trip to Delta, surviving personal business papers do not reveal. By the 1930s, when the Danish Lund family brothers Merle and Walter Lund took over the mill, subsequently opening a feed store in Paonia, Theodore and Maria's children had more options for milling their own grain as well as buying grain or flour from local stores.

In April 1893, Maria delivered her last child, a son named Theodore. But in October 1895, the eighteen-month-old child died, the result, according to the memories of his surviving siblings, of his having consumed tainted venison meat. Even before enduring this sorrow, Maria began to lose her eyesight and by the end of 1894 was already totally blind. Theodore consulted various doctors and finally took his wife to clinics in Chicago, and then to the clinic of Dr. Edward H. Bemis in Glen Falls, New York. Bemis opened his clinic, the Bemis Eye Sanatorium, in 1890—a facility which eventually included boarding houses for those coming for treatment. The average cost for treatment was $1.00 but room and board for those staying at the clinic was $7.00 per week. His sanitarium was advertised in major magazines and the newspapers of New York, Boston, and Washington, D.C. Bemis' treatment for cataracts was controversial and involved the use of a "magnetic vaporizer" which he had patented. His treatment included causing an eye hemorrhage, a procedure which followed his conviction that the blood would clear the eye of the disease which was causing blindness. In any event, Bemis did not outlive his patient Maria Roeber for long. The doctor died at the age of 52 in December 1901.

The Theodore and Maria property on German Mesa was a farm, not a ranch in the style of the vast acreages in New Mexico, Texas, or the North and South Park or San Luis Valley in Colorado. Nor was its dwelling comparable to the substantial homes of Peter Vogel or Bernard Orth. A variety of trees, including Wolf River Apples and Honey Locust Trees, had been brought from Kansas and Hollyhock flowers flanked the entry to the adobe house. But Theodore, perhaps at Maria's insistence, also recorded in detail in 1890 the planting of fruit trees and bushes on a north to south access near the house. The list included Lady, Concord, Moore's Early, Wyoming Red, and Tawney Seedless grapes; Heath Cling peaches; English morels and Olivet cherries; apricots; Wild Goose and Coe's Golden Drop plums; Early Harvest, Wealthy, Yellow Transparent, Duchess of Aldenber, Jamet, and Mit apples; Flemish Beauty, Keiffer, and Barlett pears; an "Industry" gooseberry bush; Hansell, Schaeffer, and Lucretia Danberry raspberries; and Ancient Briton blackberries, finishing with Fays Prolific and White Grape currants.

The initial cattle raised on the farm were milk stock, and the same 1890 notes show a heifer born of a milk cow; a red heifer calf, a red and white heifer calf, a red heifer calf born of "curly Range Cow," and a red and white heifer calf from a "red range cow." Galloways, a breed that originated in late seventeenth-century Scotland and was only introduced to the United States in 1882, also comprised part of the first herd. Hornless, with a shaggy coat, and commonly black, but sometimes red or dun, these cattle became the first stock which Theodore and his sons raised and sold. Some evidence survives that Galloways were also raised for milking and the making of cheese, but if so, no evidence and no family memories suggest that they were used in this way on the Roeber farm in the 1890s.

Perhaps the best way to put the initial farm into perspective is to note the role of the redoubtable Alonzo Hartman, the founder of the town of Gunnison. One of a family of five brothers, he had arrived in Colorado and begun a long career as one of the genuine "cattle barons" of the 1880s. Alonzo's younger brothers, Sam (1860-1938) and Edward, pioneered major cattle drives along a route over Black Mesa, along Crystal Creek, Curecanti Creek, and Soap Creek to a ranch they established near the town of Maher. But their search for grazing lands also took them further into the North Fork Valley and this route became known as the "Old Hartman Trail." Stories of the massive herds driven into the North Fork by these men include references to German Mesa and gallons of sour-grape wine being sold to the cowboys at the price of $1.00 a gallon. Whether the Roeber family was involved in this enterprise one cannot document. But given Theodore's decision to plant five varieties of grapes and the fact that, well into the era of Prohibition in the 1920s, the family brewed their own beer for home consumption, it seems likely that they would have taken advantage of this financial opportunity.

By 1891, a single Hartman herd numbered over 4,000 head of cattle. The last of the great herds ended in 1893. It was the growth of smaller, fenced-in farms such as the one Theodore Roeber was attempting to piece together that put an end to the massive herds, devastated the open ranges, and motivated smaller entrepreneurs to find ways to secure both land and water on a more modest, but defensible scale. The Hartman family took advantage of the expanding Denver & Rio Grande Railroad connection at Sapinero and shipped their cattle to market to Kansas City from there.

No evidence survives of the Hartman operation joining North Fork cattlemen in driving smaller herds north through the Valley and over McClure

Pass to the narrow-gauge railheads in the Crystal River Valley. Nor did the Roeber family become involved in the violent clash between cattlemen and sheepmen that erupted in the summer of 1893 with the arrival of some 6,000 head of sheep from Utah. Wilson Rockwell wrote a summary of the resulting range wars for the April 1939 issue of the Denver-based *The Westerner*—the Colorado Stock Growers and Feeders Association paper. According to Rockwell, vigilante actions were usually instigated by outsiders to avoid local cattlemen from being identified. Not until the adoption of the Taylor Grazing Act of 1934 would on-going tensions between cattle and sheep on public domain land fall "under federal supervision, thereby ending the notorious feudal warfare on the western hills and prairies."

An undated photograph—but almost certainly taken around 1894 or 1895—shows the Planer family in their home in Indiana and includes Theodore and Maria Roeber, who were on their way to New York. Estimating the ages of all seven Planer children who appear in the photograph, including the eldest son Frank, and the young Hattie and Johanne Maria, the visit must have taken place during the final years of Maria Lühring Roeber's life. The photograph documents the journey to consult specialists in Chicago and New York about Maria's failing eyesight.

By the time this photograph was taken, Theodore still boasted a full head of hair and had grown the generous moustache which he would wear for the balance of the nineteenth century. Franz Planer, his life-long friend, wore a goatee and full moustache but his hairline had receded significantly. Maria and her sister-in-law Hedwig Bertha appear in formal black dresses as does the Planer daughter Anna, who holds her sister Johanne Maria. The very young Hattie holds a formally dressed doll. Planer himself chose to appear without a coat and only a vest with pocket watch and chain, but with a proper tie. Theodore and all of the Planer boys wear ties, coats, and in some cases, vests. At some point during the 1890s, Theodore would acquire his own watch and chain and, according to the memory of his son and grandson, he purchased that "Ball Official Standard Railroad Watch" second-hand from the widow of a man who had been employed by the railroad.

Only a few private or public records survive for the years between 1889 and the late 1890s by which we can judge exactly how the expansion of the Roeber family's first acres occurred in conjunction with broader events in Colorado and the United States at the time. Theodore maintained his banking and business connections in Montrose and in 1892 addressed a letter to the Home Supply Association announcing his application for membership and asking if the agent could obtain a "3-inch Schuttler Mountain Wagon" for his use "to be picked up in Montrose as soon as possible." Theodore would have known of the Peter Schuttler Wagon Company that had been founded in Chicago in 1843 and whose several wagons included farm, freight, and mountain wagon varieties, the latter category importantly equipped with an especially robust braking system to prevent run-away accidents on mountainous grades.

With the exception of these occasional large outlays, Theodore's records of purchases are difficult to reconstruct, especially with regard to Theodore's wife Maria and her wishes regarding the furnishings of the house. An undated photograph showing a group of Colorado women standing in front of a Ute-style teepee is entitled "Ladies' Relief Corps No. 11. North Fork, Colo," in which the diminutive Maria stands dressed in her formal black dress. Years after her death, Maria's daughter-in-law, Fannie Alderson, was told by Theodore that he had to call Maria into the house when guests arrived, telling her "...you must not work, you must come in and visit" to which she would reply, *"die Arbeit, die Arbeit."*

The furnishings within the family's modest two-room cabin-plus-attic sleeping area included Theodore's framed copy of his GAR discharge paper; his transfer from the Kansas GAR Post; and the much larger certificate of his appointment as Inspector to the GAR Department of Colorado and Wyoming. There was also a framed picture of himself, his wife and their first two children, and possibly the framed photograph of his acquaintance, Aaron Clough. Clough was a settler who had first gained respect as a wagon train scout and guide before retiring to a life of farming and ranching. By 1895–97, the cabin's wall also featured framed certificates of Theodore's candidacy with the Silver Republicans as well as his successful election and appointment as County Assessor. In September of 1896, Theodore attended the Montrose

Western Slope GAR Veterans' Association meeting, a practice that became increasingly a part of his annual life, especially after the death of his spouse.

Theodore's insistence that his children acquire a basic literacy and attend schools had already been demonstrated in Kansas and, briefly, during the Roeber family's year in the Maple Grove settlement near Montrose. Theodore would show the same keen interest in the North Fork Valley schools, eventually helping to support and serve on the board of a new "District Five" rural school district, located a few miles to the north of his property in Dry Gulch—a place which was aptly named for its lack of water except for that used by Levi Miller, another German-speaking settler whose farm lay at the eastern edge of the area.

It is not possible to date exactly when Theodore acquired the books that would comprise the modest library of his and Maria's home. *The History of the Ninth Regiment Illinois Cavalry Volunteers,* published in Chicago in 1888, was one of them. An 1893 memorial edition of the *Life and Work of James G. Blaine,* the Republican Senator from Maine and unsuccessful candidate for the Presidency, found a place on a shelf, along with the *Pictorial History of Our War with Spain for Cuba's Freedom.* The 1896 two-volume *History of the United States* by R. Benjamin Andrews may have completed the volumes on public or political life. On one of Theodore's trips to visit his relatives in Indiana and Illinois, or possibly while taking part in one of the larger GAR reunions, he brought home the *Camp Fire Entertainment* and *True History of Robert Henry Hendershot the Drummer Boy of the Rappahannock* by H.E. Gerry. Published in Chicago in 1903, that volume included the words, and in some cases the musical notations, for various patriotic songs.

Of far more practical importance was Theodore's copy of S.W. Carpenter's *The Law of Water for Irrigation in Colorado* published in Denver in 1887: "Containing all the Legislation adopted by the Colorado General Assembly, Session of 1887, and all additional decisions down to May 15th, 1887, etc." So too was the 1891 volume *The Peoples Farm and Stock Cyclopedia.* Theodore's possession of Mark Twain's 1897 *Following the Equator* suggests at least some interest and acquaintance with the great American humorist's writing.

No German-language books, secular or religious, appear to have been purchased or bequeathed to Theodore and Maria's children. Nor did Theodore and Maria replace the Roeber family bible that was destroyed in the 1873 fire in Indiana. The inside cover of a copy of Luther's *Small Catechism* bears the inscription: "Maria Lühring Junior" suggesting that Theodore's wife had been gifted this version of the Catechism prior to her marriage, perhaps when she was confirmed. According to a royal decree of 14 April 1862, the Catechism had been published in Lüneburg, Germany, for the churches and schools of the Kingdom of Hannover. Another copy of the Catechism, bound with a few hymns, reveals a cover that has been laboriously stitched together and includes the signature of Theodore and Maria's oldest son, Frank.

By contrast, Theodore and Maria's oldest daughter, Mary, had been gifted, in 1886, with a German-language volume published in Philadelphia in 1884—a book which provided a "biblical history" for young people, including a brief account of the history of the Christian church to 1648. In 1897, The Reverend Virgil Thompson made a present in March of that year to the young Mary Roeber of an English Bible complete with the attached *Bible Readers' Aids* by Charles H.H. Wright. Many years later, after her 1926 marriage to Joseph Brown, who later died in 1930, "Mary Braun" received a copy of a German-language Lutheran Catechism from "her Anty Maria Luehring 83 years old," Hanover, Kansas—the inscription dated June 25, 1934. Mary's devotion to the faith of her parents was also obvious in a hand-embroidered and gilt-framed picture which had its place on her bedroom wall. It depicts an angel with the German inscription: *"An Gottes Segen ist Alles gelegen."* (Everything rests upon God's blessing.)

One other aspect of the Roeber family's early domestic life that remains unclear surrounds the playing of musical instruments. No evidence survives of either Theodore or Maria having learned to play or sing. Yet, by the time their children began to reach adulthood, a guitar, a mandolin, banjo, harmonica, and a violin were all acquired. Theodore's third son, Otto, was credited as being the lover of music. Otto, along with his younger brother, Louie, taught himself to play all these instruments, although the violin was his favorite and the instrument he regularly played at dances. Although no purchase dates can be identified for when the instruments were acquired, the surviving instruments appear to have been ordered from Sears, Roebuck and Company catalogues and shipped to Colorado via mail-order from Chicago.

Theodore joined the International Order of Odd Fellows and the Benevolent and Protective Order of Elks—affiliations which perhaps came about as part of his ambitions for public life which resulted in his assuming the office of County Assessor in 1895 and again in 1897. The framed and signed certificates of office found their places on the walls of his home. During his time as Assessor, Theodore needed help in executing his duties. Since his wife had lost her sight and never learned to speak or read English with any fluency, his daughter Elizabeth (affectionately called Lizzie), who had learned the skills of bookkeeping, served as Theodore's secretary. Elizabeth accompanied him to Delta when his duties called for such travel. She assisted him until May 1899, when she married Joseph William Humphrey who had been employed on Theodore's farm. In recognition of Lizzie's aid to him during his years as Assessor, on December 4, 1897, Theodore bought her a gift for which he kept the receipt. That receipt came from Nellie Carver of Delta who declared: "I hereby bargain, sell & Convey to Theodore Roeber one Organ named the Western Cottage, for the sum of $40.00 Cash." The "Western Cottage" pump organ was a reed organ made by a company that had begun in 1865, moving from Mendota to Ottawa, Illinois, and eventually branching out into pianos until the factory burned and the company went out of business in the early twentieth century.

The survival of photographs taken of the family from the 1860s onward must be credited to the devotion of Maria Lühring Roeber. She preserved those images in a handsomely worked and leather-bound photograph album, gilt-edged, and with floral illustrations providing a border surrounding the individual pictures. The album contained photographs of Theodore's mother, his sisters and their families—including some of the families of Bertha's illegitimate children. It also included several photographs of the Lühring family in Kansas. Since the trunk in which many of the family valuables were transported to Colorado also survived, one can surmise that Maria kept the album in this trunk, or, perhaps, it occupied a place on the shelf of books in the home.

Whether Maria had a major voice in the purchases her husband made for the home is unclear. Cancelled checks and Theodore's application to be accepted as a member of the Paonia Marketing Association reveal glimpses of where and how he conducted business during the first ten years of the family's life on German Mesa. Small checks ranging from a dollar to twenty dollars went to neighbors and business associates. Other checks appear in surviving check stubs drawn on the Delta County Treasurer during his work as Assessor. Names on the stubs include Weldon Hammond, Frederick Lukas, Basheba Quackenbush, Peter Vogel, M.P. Gonner, Levi Miller, and Samuel Wade—all early and, in some cases, prominent settlers in the North Fork Valley.

Theodore paid a considerable sum—$43.50—to the "American Steel Scraper Co." presumably to acquire the equipment needed to clear his lands of rocks, sagebrush, and juniper stumps—or possibly to aid in the construction of the irrigation ditch that ran from the Lake Fork of Minnesota Creek over five miles to his property. He had become acquainted with the machinery of the McCormick Company during his youth in Indiana and Illinois. Surviving implements on the ranch include a horse-drawn mowing machine carrying the McCormick-Deering trademark—the result of the merger of McCormick and Deering Harvester Companies into the International Harvester Company by 1902.

Theodore also paid various sums to his sons Frank and Otto for work done on a variety of irrigation projects. These included the ditch delivering Clark and Wade water as well as the purchase of a half cubic foot of water from Reynold's Creek to the south of his original property to help irrigate tracts of land which he added to the original 80 acres. He wrote a large check for $150 in 1893 to his future son-in-law, Joseph Brown, who worked on the farm. In 1896, he issued a $5.00 check to his eldest daughter, Mary—perhaps as payment for her having given up a position as housemaid for George Sampson in Montrose in order to return home to care for her blind mother, a task she filled until Maria's death in 1901.

Occasionally, a major purchase was made, along with many smaller checks that were written to the store of Goodenow & Swan, the dry goods and furnishings store in Paonia as well as Duke Brothers & Co. in the town that offered "groceries, clothing, hats and caps, boots and shoes, hardware, hardwood, Queensware, agricultural implements, buggies and wagons and builders' material." By August of 1889, Theodore subscribed to the *Delta Independent* newspaper. He also paid his dues to the North Fork Post 86 of the GAR and his yearly taxes to the Delta County Treasurer—an obligation which ranged from $14.75 in 1893, to $33.40 a year later in 1894.

As the aforementioned 1899 description of German Mesa revealed, and the listing of fruit trees and bushes confirms, the Roeber property was known initially as much for its orchards as for its stock of cattle. Although a member of the Paonia Fruit Growers' Association, Theodore's interest in other ventures increased during the 1890s. During this time, his attention was focused on his cattle, his irrigation projects, and the expansion of land on which cattle could graze or on which hay crops could be grown to sustain cattle during the winter months. His interest in the sustenance of his cattle was especially profound after 1893 when the grazing of cattle across unfenced lands in the Valley came to a close.

Regarding water, Theodore served as president of the Turner Ditch Company, and with a large group of optimistic neighbors, he also participated in the construction of the Mount Lamborn Ditch, a huge—and ultimately failed—attempt to bring water from springs several miles to the south. Had the project succeeded, it would have joined with the spring that fed what was first known as Quackenbush Creek which ran through the property. (Quackenbush was later renamed Bell Creek for a subsequent settler.) By the late 1940s, the pasture and water rights would be acquired by the town of Paonia from the estate of Edward Bates, hence the "Town Pasture." These plans to irrigate otherwise arid and barren mesas and farms that abutted Theodore's property to the south never developed. Thus, he had to be content with irrigating those parts of his lands by acquiring water rights in Reynolds Creek between his property and that of Frank (not Frederick) Lukas.

Just how critical water rights remained in this high desert valley area became clear when the case of *Vogel v. Minnesota Canal and Reservoir Company et al* reached the Colorado Supreme Court in 1909. Peter Vogel, the man who had bought land and water rights first from Bernard Orth had brought suit which had failed in Superior Court. The suit proposed to change part of the diversion of water further upstream from the headgate of the Clark & Wade ditch to the Turner ditch four miles further upstream and "the residue to the Beaver Dam ditch of seven miles higher," i.e., Theodore Roeber's ditch. The court found, however, that if this were to happen, those landowners further downstream who had arrived later in the Valley and were now attempting to grow crops late in the summer would have no water available to them at all; the right of prior use—the basic premise of riparian rights—had limitations—and changing the manner in which water was diverted initially from a spring or creek bed was one of those limitations. Notice of the suit appeared in the September 1897 issue of the *Delta Independent,* alerting interested parties to the importance of the deliberations.

Theodore diligently sought to obtain water rights and expand his property holdings to ensure a contiguous set of acquisitions thereby forestalling small 40-acre purchases which were allowed after 1905—rather than the previous requirement to patent 160 acres of Federal land. And yet, while focusing on water, he also developed a Colorado connection for marketing his cattle. It is not clear why Theodore chose at first to do business with particular cattle buyers in Omaha, Nebraska, although he may have known the Omaha firm from his time in Kansas. The earliest surviving bills and correspondence show that his cattle were driven with those of other stock growers north through the valley and over McClure Pass to the narrow-gauge railhead at Placita, or alternatively over Kebler Pass toward Crested Butte and the railheads at Floresta or Baldwin.

The first shipment of cattle from the Roeber farm that made its way to Omaha was accomplished in 1893. Using the services of Waggoner, Birney & Company, Theodore sold his cattle to Cudahy & Company for slaughter at the rate of $2.75 per hundred-weight. By 1895, however, Theodore had switched to doing business with R.H. Barnes & Co. Livestock Commission Merchants at the Denver Union Stockyards. A surviving receipt reveals that, by 1896, R.H. Barnes had been succeeded by the "Sigel-Barnes Stock Commission Company headed by F.L. Sigel." Thus, in 1899, Theodore used Sigel-Barnes as commissioners to sell his 33 steers to the *Hammond Brothers.*

After paying freight, yardage, hay and the commission costs, Theodore's net proceeds came to $1,153.08.

With the foregoing 1899 transaction, the Roeber saga seemed to come full-circle because *Hammond Brothers* were the very same firm which, years before, had constructed an enormous meat-packing plant which rejuvenated an Indiana town near the original land which the patriarch Christian Roeber had purchased in 1854.

Oral history passed down by Theodore's son, Gustave, hints at the reason for the change in the commissioners to whom Theodore entrusted his cattle. Gustave recalled his father telling him that Mr. Sigel, their buyer in Denver, could speak German, and that it was important to do business with him early in the day when he would be more inclined to work hard for a good sale price for the cattle. Gustave also related a less attractive part of the family's oral history—a reflection of the long tensions between Jewish and Christian communities in Europe. Gustave recalled that Mr. Sigel was Jewish and known to drive an increasingly hard bargain as the business day unfolded.

It may be a reflection of the quality of Theodore's stock that other commissioners chose to bid for Roeber cattle. The American Livestock & Loan Company sent a Happy New Year card, and the firm of Clay, Robinson & Company sent a large photograph of the "Stocker and Feeder Exhibit of 1909 at the National Western Stock Show." This yearly exhibit, sale, and rodeo was favored by members of the Stockman's Club founded in 1906 and of which Theodore became an early member. He continued to pay his dues to the Stockmen's Club in Denver throughout the remaining years of his life, and secured passes for his sons to attend, although whether and how often this actually happened remains unclear.

By 1898, as his wife's condition worsened, Theodore may have been disinclined for family reasons to continue serving as County Assessor. But events on September 7, 1898, in Colorado Springs may also have contributed to his retirement from public office. *The Press Democrat* of 10 September 1898 reported a riot which broke out between two factions of the Silver Republicans on September 7th resulting in the deaths of several men. The National Committee of the Silver Republicans had removed Richard Broad from serving as chair of the state committee, according to his critics, for his having joined

Senator Edward O. Wolcott in a conspiracy to "defeat the proposed fusion with the Democrats and Populists" which was intended to stand against McKinley Republicans. Wolcott, born in 1848, a GAR veteran and Harvard Law School graduate had served as Republican state senator from 1879 to 1882 and was then elected to the U.S. Senate in 1889 and again in 1895. Sympathetic to the position of the Silver Republicans, Wolcott nonetheless was regarded by at least some to have been responsible for the defeat of the proposed fusion. He lost his seat in the Senate in 1901 to Thomas Patterson, the Democrat who served from 1901 to 1909. No surviving correspondence either from or to Theodore reveals to what extent the events in Colorado Springs and the national elections influenced his political views.

Among the items Theodore kept in the small leather pocketbook that included the copy of his birth certificate, a German-language newspaper notice found its place along with a small plait of his wife Maria's hair. The German-language clip read "We inform the many friends and acquaintances here of Mrs. Heckelmann on her behalf that her daughter in law Mrs. Maria Roeber during these last days in Dolton Co. Col. *[Delta County, Colorado]* at the age of 51 years has died. Mrs. Roeber has been blind for 20 years and her death occurred as a result of brain cancer *(Gehirnverzehrung)* that was the cause of her blindness. The deceased was treated by the most eminent specialists of ophthalmology in Chicago and New York, without results. The pitiable one had, without complaint to accept her fate and wished for nothing more ardently than her release by death from her suffering and torment." Dying on July 16, 1901, Maria Lühring Roeber was 51 years, nine months and 24 days old.

Even before his wife's death, Theodore's children had begun to disperse. With the sole exception of his daughter Clara, his children would marry neither a fellow Lutheran, nor a speaker of German; neither his son Otto nor Louis ever married and the marriages of some of his daughters ended in separation or divorce. Even had the anti-German sentiments that sprang up during the First World War and directly targeted the residents of German Mesa never occurred, the Roeber children born in the United States appear to have been typical of nearly all "second generation" Americans who were not interested, for the most part, in keeping alive the language, faith, and family customs brought by their parents to North America. Or, as subsequent events and recollections revealed, they had endured too many taunts as children about their accents and were determined as adults to put the ethnic identity of their parents behind them. Both the sequence of his children's marriages, coupled with a remarkable silence surrounding his eldest son Frank, help to explain why the twentieth-century history of Theodore and Maria's family would be dominated by the work and personality of their second-oldest surviving son, Gustave Wilhelm.

From a German American father born into the Kingdom of Saxony who was familiar with the practice in Saxon law for settling estates on the first-born eldest son, one would have expected Theodore to have seen Frank Leonard—the eldest and named for Theodore's closest friend Franz Planer—playing the key role of heir apparent. A striking example of what *did not happen* can be seen in the brands for cattle that Theodore and his sons registered with the State of Colorado. They secured four different brands, and in addition to the one he used, each of the remaining three belonged to sons Gustave, Otto, and Louis—but none for Frank. That Frank did not come to play the role one would have expected may have had something to do with the strained relationship Theodore seemed to have had with both his eldest children.

His eldest daughter, Mary Augusta, had gone to school in Kansas and lived with the Weyer (Lühring) family because she did not get along with her father. Although she had moved to German Mesa from the Montrose area, she returned there unmarried in the early 1890s coming home only to care for her mother. A year before her mother's death in 1901, Mary returned to the Montrose region. There, she met Edward Sellars, marrying him in March 1902 in a ceremony held at her sister Elizabeth's home. "Lizzie" herself had married Joseph William Humphrey in May of 1899 and the couple lived briefly with her parents, Theodore and Maria, while Humphrey finished building a cabin on the most westward 40 acres of the Roeber property—a tract of land which Theodore had gifted to his daughter.

Mary's marriage lasted barely more than a year, and she returned to the North Fork Valley with an infant daughter. Her own 40 acres of land, which she had received upon her marriage, she sold to her brothers Frank and Gus, and her brother-in-law Charles Wiening in 1909, in exchange for the purchase of a small house in the town of Paonia. In 1911, she re-named her daughter "Nola May" Dorothy Marie and had the child baptized in the Lutheran faith with her aunts Lizzie and Clara as sponsors. It may have been the case that this early failed marriage further strained relationships between Mary and her father, circumstances which may account for Theodore's granddaughter Dorothy Sellars' recollection of her grandfather as "not a nice man."

Mary's younger sister, Clara Catherine, was the only one of Theodore and Maria's children to marry a fellow German-speaking Lutheran, Charles Frederick Wiening, on November 20, 1900, in a Lutheran service held in the county seat, Delta. But unlike her siblings, Clara did not stay on the 40 acres given to her by her father—a site which adjoined her sister Lizzie's farm on the east. Instead, she and her husband returned to Illinois. This wedding also saw a reunion of Theodore with his nephew Louis Planer, who came West for the occasion. The Wiening family were descended from the immigrant Joseph Wiening, who died in 1885, and whose descendants had also settled in the same areas of Indiana and Illinois as did the Planer and Roeber families. One of Charles Wiening's brothers, Christ Wiening, married Mary Planer (1871–1954)—a union which further cemented the relationships among the three families.

In the years following Maria's death, some of the Roeber children returned to the family fold. After two years in Illinois, Charles and Clara Wiening returned to Colorado to live with Theodore from 1903 to 1905 while Charles completed building a log cabin on the Wiening's own acreage, to which 28 acres were added by Theodore. By 1905, Theodore and Mary's daughter Margarete "Maggie" had also moved to Crawford, Colorado, and a year later had married Edward Piburn in 1906. This marriage also failed, and Maggie was forced to sell the property given to her by her father to her brother-in-law Charles Wiening.

The youngest Roeber daughter, Augusta Juliana, was only 11 when her mother died. As a child, she had tried to help her blind mother, taking her for walks along Lukas Creek which ran near the family's house. Augusta's childhood was spent either in her father's home or those of her older married sisters, Clara and Lizzie. From her 15th year she, like her sisters before her, went to work as a hired girl in various jobs. Married at age 19 in 1908, she and William Ruble would have eight children, live briefly in a one-room cabin on the property she received from Theodore, but then move to Peach Valley, where her marriage, like that of more than one of her siblings, was fated to fail by the mid-1920s. Raising her children by herself, "Gusty" eventually married a second time in 1954 to James Arthur Hill and spent the balance of her life in Austin, Colorado, until her death in 1968—the last of Theodore and Maria's children.

An undated clipping from the *Delta County Independent* entitled "Know Your Neighbor" by Hazel Austin recorded Augusta's recollections of her life. It is possible that the interviewer misunderstood Gusty or failed to accurately record what she had been told as a child about her parents. But Gusty's story of her father Theodore, at age 14, traveling to America with her grandfather Christian and her recollection that they were "14 months crossing the Atlantic" was clearly wrong (more likely, she meant 14 weeks). It is equally implausible that a later crossing by Maria Lühring Roeber and her family caused them to spend 10 months at sea. Nor was it true that her parents married in Kansas. What sounds more accurate was Augusta's account of the move from Kansas to Paonia. According to Gusty, Theodore and Frank "came in the emigrant car with the mules, machinery, furniture and the peacocks" while Theodore's wife and other children came by regular passenger train. The constricted "emigrant car" of the 1840s had evolved from its rudimentary dimensions to a more elaborate vehicle that included space for animals plus simple berths but also kitchens where passengers could prepare their own meals. Food and blankets were the responsibility of the passengers unless they wished to pay extra for having the railroad provide these items. Gusty's memory of being ridiculed for her German and her German-inflected English, however, rings true as does her account of being delighted to have an adult conversation with a German-speaking woman. "This experience of conversing with a lonesome German lady helped to make up to Augusta for all the taunts and slights of her childhood and made her glad that she had learned her parents' mother tongue."

Theodore appears to have put little thought into providing education and financial stability for his youngest children, especially the girls. What aspirations or expectations he had for his four sons remain also in part a matter of considerable speculation. As it happens, the 20th century history of the Roeber family in the North Fork Valley of the Gunnison River centers on the person and work of Theodore's second son, Gustave. Therefore, his aspirations and disappointments will dominate Chapter Four of this present history. So, it is sufficient here to note that, during the 1890s when this son was only ten years of age, his father had already begun to rely on him to herd cattle and acquire the knowledge he would need to succeed Theodore as heir.

The portrait of Theodore, Maria, and their nine surviving children which appears on the cover of this book was taken some time *after* Maria's death—an earlier photograph of her was added to complete the portrait. That photo shows the oldest son Frank standing between his sister Mary and his younger brother Gustave. Frank wears the identical moustache sported by his father, has parted his hair exactly like Theodore, and stands directly behind his father. Despite being, arguably, the most handsome of the brothers—as the cattle herd grew and the business of farming increased in complexity—Frank did not emerge in the 1890s as the person upon whom his father relied.

An incident which the children managed to keep secret from their father provides some insight into Frank's shortcomings. When the family was in New York, as a young man of about twenty, Frank had entered the house during his parents' absence to find his younger siblings playing in the kitchen. Picking up a gun he mistakenly thought was unloaded, he pointed the gun at his sister Lizzie and (presumably in German) called out "ready, aim, fire" and carelessly sent a bullet through his sister's hair (she wore it in a bun on top of her head.) To conceal the evidence, a nail was driven into the wall and an old overcoat hung upon it in an apparent attempt to keep Theodore and Maria from learning what had happened. If Frank was capable of such a feckless act as a young man in his twenties, perhaps the incident pointed to a broader lack of judgment or ambition—limitations which may have caused Theodore to bypass his eldest son as he worked to expand his property, its orchards, and herds during the first decade of the Roeber family's life in the North Fork Valley.

Frank would not marry until his 38th year, in 1912. When he did so, he married Mary Alderson Allebaugh, a young widow. Theodore had done occasional business with Daniel Allebaugh, who had been born in Ohio before moving to Illinois, then to Iowa, and ultimately, by 1893, to the North Fork Valley of Colorado. Allebaugh's son, Ernest W., born in 1876, had married Mary Alderson but died at the age of 33, leaving behind his widow and three children. Between 1909 and 1911, Daniel Allebaugh's family and Ernest's had moved to Caldwell, Idaho, and, after the death of her husband, Mary Allebaugh had returned to the North Fork Valley home of her parents, Samuel and Mary Caroline Alderson. Three years later, she married Frank Roeber.

With the help of his brother-in-law, Charles Wiening, Frank built a cabin on property he had received from his father—at a site next to lands owned by his sisters. The difficulty of raising a family on land only marginally suited for cultivation forced Frank to go to work by 1918 as a hired hand for a larger ranch. The ranch was situated on arid lands further to the south and in a region which had acquired the ominous name "Bone Mesa."

Frank may have had his faults, but he seemed determined to make a go of things. In a notebook kept by Gustave (Gus) for the year 1909—in a time before Frank's marriage—Frank's brother noted that, although Frank had not worked on the construction of the Inner Ocean ditch (later known as the Lone Cabin) he was hired to walk the length of the ditch from mid-July to late August of that year. According to Gus' notes, the reason for this task was because on June 30th the "ditch brock *[broke]* about 500 yards below Reservoir."

In 1920, Frank put his original cabin on skids and with a team of horses, moved it some miles to the north—positioning it only a mile or so to the west of a ranch worked by his younger brother, Gus. Though he tried, Frank appears never to have found farming or ranching to be profitable or promising. By 1923, he was working as a day laborer in the town of Paonia to which he had moved. Two years later, in 1925, he moved with his wife, three adopted children, and three sons born to him and Mary to Idaho, again as a hired laborer. By 1926, Frank had moved to Chehalis, Washington, to work in a lumber mill. His job there lasted six years. Diagnosed with cancer in late 1932, Frank died in February 1933.

In his own remarks about his early years, one of Frank's sons shared his recollections of his father. Philip Roeber recalled attending one-room rural schools until the age of 12. He remembered his "family constantly moving from one sharecropping farm to another" until the family left Colorado in 1926 "bound for Idaho, but continued on, in a kind of pre-Joad family move, to the Pacific Northwest, Lewis County, western Washington State." By 1929, the timber industry and small towns went bankrupt, "mills were burned down, and much of the housing...mill towns became ghost towns." For Philip, the years 1930 to 1936 were remembered as the "gradual disintegration of the family" with the death of his father in 1933 and that of his younger brother in 1936.

Considering this sad tale, one is tempted to ask whether Frank had perhaps suffered as a child some injury that impeded his intellectual development or burdened him with a physical ailment which prevented him from engaging in the demanding labor necessary to wring a living out of a harsh landscape. The fact that such sicknesses did afflict two of his younger brothers lends at least the color of plausibility to such speculation.

His younger brothers, Adolph Christian (Otto) and Ludwig Heinrich (Louie) both suffered as children from serious diseases. At times, Otto exhibited uncontrolled jerking and tremors which suggest that he had been infected as a child, during a bout with rheumatic fever, with Sydenham's chorea, commonly known as "Saint Vitus' Dance." Despite these challenges, Otto worked his own property and cattle and on occasion as a reliable hand on the Frank Smith spread and other area ranches. He suffered a serious accident when a stump-puller mal-functioned causing the handles of the winch to strike him so hard that for the rest of his life he could only sleep in a sitting position. The youngest brother, Louis, contracted typhoid fever at the age of 15, two years after his mother's death and recovered largely due to the care given him by his younger sister, Augusta, who followed the instructions given her by Theodore. In both instances, these men remained unmarried, but actively involved on modestly successful properties that featured the combination of farming, ranching, and work on irrigation projects. Louis served in World War I and—though sources offer differing accounts—he either died in France or succumbed to Influenza while enroute to the war. In any event, he was reported missing and ultimately declared dead on October 5, 1918. His name appears on the Tablets of the Missing at Suresnes American Cemetery, Suresnes, France. His siblings first received notice of his death at sea from the War Department, only to be shaken a few weeks later by the arrival of a postcard from France in his hand telling them that he had arrived. The most likely explanation appears to be that he had already died at sea and the mail reached his relatives only after they had been informed of his death. Apparently these two brothers overcame their circumstances and achieved some measure of success, unlike the wandering career of their older brother Frank.

The ability to harvest and sell both fruit and cattle from the farms and ranches of the North Fork Valley changed dramatically by 1902–03. William Jackson Palmer, the head of the Denver & Rio Grande Railroad (until his removal in 1901 from the Presidency of the line he had founded) learned of the discovery of major coal seams north of Gunnison that gave rise to the town of Crested Butte a few miles to the northeast of the North Fork Valley in Gunnison County. Although coal mined there initially helped supply fuel for silver mining camps, Palmer recognized that the production of coke that could fuel the Colorado Coal and Iron Company in which Palmer was a major investor argued for the extension of the railroad into these areas. Despite the bad reputation of the Crested Butte mine, due to the infamous 1884 Jokerville Mine explosion that killed 59 miners, the Colorado Fuel and Iron Company opened the Big Mine in Crested Butte shortly thereafter. Ultimately, the Big Mine produced the majority of the coal sent east over Marshall Pass to the Colorado Fuel and Iron steel mills at Pueblo.

Although the early settlers in the North Fork of the Gunnison Valley had discovered small outcroppings of coal in the 1880s, Palmer also learned that large seams of coal lay at the far northern end of the valley. By 1902, even after Palmer's departure from the Denver & Rio Grande, its officers and stakeholders opted to build a narrow-gauge line laid over the 30 miles from Delta to Paonia. The line also extended beyond Paonia for an additional 15 miles to an area which Palmer had bought and where he established the town of Somerset. (Somerset lay in Gunnison County but, due to topography and transportation challenges, was effectively cut off from that county for years.) The rails for this North Fork branch line of the Denver & Rio Grande's main western line between Salida and Grand Junction were laid on a bed that enabled the line to be changed from narrow- to standard-gauge a year later.

The use of the railroad to export large shipments of both fruit and cattle accelerated the economic development of the Valley, but it was coal that had attracted Palmer's interest in the first place, not the agricultural products of the Valley. Much of the coal mined in Bowie, Somerset, and later the Hawks' Nest Mine where the rail line ended, provided fuel for local homes and businesses. Most of the men who found employment in the mines worked seasonally—in the Winter in the mines, and on their small farms during the Spring, Summer, and early Fall. A core group of miners kept the mines open and operational year-round and, as demand increased, so too did year-round employment for many families in the North Fork Valley. The expansion of the coal mines in the Valley aided the Roeber family indirectly. The mines, the Somerset Boarding House, and the availability of small farms as well as the need for labor provided employment at one time or another, for Theodore and Maria's children: Mary, Louis, Maggie, and Gusty.

By 1903, Theodore began a pattern of travel that became a yearly routine from that time until his death in 1916. In 1903, he made the trip by railroad to St. Louis for the famed Exposition that celebrated the Louisiana Purchase and the "opening of the West" by Lewis and Clark. As a memento of the Exposition, he received, by mail from *The Kansas City Journal,* a facsimile reproduction of the scene entitled "Golgotha" by the Polish artist, Jan Styka (1858–1925.) Styka had originally painted the scene on a canvas so large that its intended exhibition at the St. Louis World Fair had to be cancelled. The lithograph reproduction Theodore received remained, however, rolled up in the tube in which it arrived; he never mounted or framed it.

In another nod to the media of the day, around the year 1900 Theodore also purchased a stereoscope from the firm of Underwood & Underwood—an enterprise founded in Kansas by the brothers Elmer and Bert Underwood in 1881. By 1900, the successful business began to offer boxed sets of scenes that could be viewed through the stereoscope. Theodore's collection included one of the life of Christ, one of American natural scenes, a third of American army life scenes that appear to reflect the U.S. army around the time of the Spanish-American War, and a final collection of European capitals and famous landmarks.

Theodore had already travelled in 1901 as far as Detroit, Michigan, for the Memorial Day observances of the GAR in that city. More local veterans' meetings in Montrose and Grand Junction in 1902 and 1903 required his attendance in his role as Inspector for the Colorado and Wyoming Department of the GAR. Increasingly, Theodore turned over the management of his cattle and property to his second son, Gus, although penciled notes in surviving books show that he remained very much in control of the continued expansion of his ranch.

In addition to the influence of coal, a second major change in the public life of the North Fork Valley residents occurred with the founding of newspapers. The independent *Gazette* began publication in 1900 followed by the Republican *Paonia Booster* in 1904; the Democratic *Paonia Newspaper* in the same year, and eventually *The Paonian* in 1911—as well as the short-lived *North Fork Times*—together creating a surfeit of printed matter for a town and surrounding area that numbered only a few hundred persons. Early in his years in the Valley, Theodore had subscribed to the countywide publication, the *Delta Independent;* whether he added a subscription to the local Republican newspaper remains unclear.

In November of 1905, Theodore received a letter from his brother-in-law Nicholas Steinbach who informed Theodore that his mother Bertha, had been killed by an express Nickel Plate train at the State Street crossing in

Hammond, Indiana. Steinbach's (only partially legible) German letter related the shocking tale: as family members began their Christmas shopping in Chicago, Bertha had visited various members of the family, then crossed the tracks and been caught by the urban train's cowcatcher which threw her back, breaking her leg in three places, shattering her shoulder and arm, and leaving a major head wound as well. She died soon thereafter, after which an inquest was held. Some years earlier, Bertha had become a member of St. Paul's Lutheran Church in Hammond, an initially independent congregation that had recently become a member of the Evangelical German-Lutheran Church of Missouri and Other States. Her membership card recorded her as "Bertha Roeber (Heckelmann) born in *Lungwitz Königreich Sachsen.*" A coffin had been purchased and the funeral service held, with Steinbach noting that burial was difficult because of the frozen ground.

The Lake County News recorded the incident on November 9, 1905, noting that the accident occurred on election day. According to this account, "in full view of many horrified spectators" the 11:20 Nickel Plate east-bound train came through the town with the gates that had already been lowered. "It is asserted that Mrs. Heckleman got under the gate to cross the track to hurry across the many railway crossings at that point. She was on her way to Hohman street. The engineer saw her about to cross the tracks and blew his whistle. The tender of the big locomotive picked up the old woman and slammed her with crushing force that her body rebounded and fell in the right of way. The train was stopped before it reached the Sibley Street crossing…her face was a sickening sight when her prostrate and bleeding body was picked up by the male spectators…she was taken to her home, 405 Indiana Ave. where she resides with the family of her son, Louis Heckleman… Dr. C.W. Campbell attended the victim at her home and worked with her for several hours. It is feared she cannot recover."

Theodore had never enjoyed a close relationship with his mother although he did apparently include her in his visits to Indiana and Illinois to see his sisters and his close friend Franz Planer. Now, with Bertha's death coming four years after the death of his wife, and with three of his five daughters now married, his domestic life became increasingly shaped by his relationship with his sons. In February 1913, he would also learn of the death of his sister Augusta, narrowing still further the number of women and family members in his life.

In 1907, he travelled to Chicago for the 9th Illinois Cavalry Reunion in October, beginning a pattern of leaving his ranch, especially during the winter months when his lung trouble—which he always described as "asthma"—apparently worsened. In 1909 and 1910, he would attend GAR gatherings in Trinidad, Colorado, and take a "Colorado Special" train to a National Encampment in Utah, and again, in 1911, make the journey to Chicago for the 25th 9th Illinois Cavalry Reunion. Theodore was travelling in the American Southeast in the Fall of 1912 and apparently missed the GAR encampment in Los Angeles.

In January 1913, Theodore received New Year's greetings from Julius Heidenreich of Morgan Park, Illinois, who informed him that he had "been in Europe all summer & returned 1st September and then immediately went to the Encampment at Los Angeles and sorry to say came right by your place or very near it. I came home last of November."

The last invitation Theodore received was to attend the August 1915, 29th reunion of the 9th Illinois Cavalry held in Chicago—but he did not attend. Theodore kept all of his reunion badges along with his commemorative badge of the St. Louis Exposition, a German American association badge and his Colorado Stock Growers' badge mounted, framed and under glass on the wall of his home. A much larger 5.5 by 1.5-foot panoramic photograph of the Trinidad GAR reunion joined the smaller collection of badges.

Theodore's interest in the orchards on his property declined during the first decade of the new century. The town of Paonia was incorporated in 1902, would build its own high school two years later, and because of the prosperity derived from mines, orchards, and livestock, would grow by 1910 to just over 1,000 persons—a level it would not attain again until after World War II.

Theordore's continuing focus on the cattle, water rights, and acquisition of other properties turned out to be wise. Both the climate of the North Fork Valley, and the absence of insects had guaranteed the growth and prosperity of the Valley's economy from the late 1880s until 1910. By the latter date, however, infestations of pests, including the Codling Moth, a glutted market the previous year, and a devastating freeze in 1912 put an end to the bumper crops of apples, peaches, pears, and cherries that had won reputations for quality—accolades which had garnered for local orchardists Samuel Wade and W.S. Coburn six first place ribbons at the Chicago World's Fair of 1902. Ironically, at just the time when the fruit industry was beginning its decline, the February 1, 1912 issue of *The Paonia Booster* reproduced from *Harper's Weekly* a January 20th photograph identifying for a national audience: "The North Fork Valley fruit district, showing the town of Paonia."

The surviving notebooks carried by Theodore and his son Gustav demonstrate that the Roeber family enterprises had local client buyers for their increasingly more important sources of income, namely: hogs, wheat, and cattle. The occasional letter survives, and these also reveal the increasing trust other cattlemen put in Theodore's sons. A 1909 postcard addressed to "Mr. Louis Roeber" implored him: "Louie, if your father has any wheat to sell tell him to bring us 100 pounds by the first of April and oblige Olive Small." Gus received a letter from Hotchkiss, Colorado, in April of that year from an unidentified (but clearly German American) correspondent addressing him as "Mr. Guss Robert" and informing him that "well guess i turned out 32 head of cattle on quackenbusch creek and would like to have you look out for them. Ther is 2 milch *[milk]* cow, one is a big read *[red]* cow that has not got eny ear mark and the other is not ear marked and when they have calves bleas *[please]* get them in and let me no and I will com and get them."

In September of 1909, Theodore was in Hammond, Indiana, writing his "Dear Son Gustave" that his health was "first rate. I have been buggie riding every day this week been drinking beer every day and gained 4 lb since I came here…how is the hay did any of the hay spoil any from the rain. I think I will stay here until the first week in October, that is if you can get along without me. Louie your cosin is out Treshing *[threshing grain]*. I have been out to see him it is an all-steel machine… I can't get no stopover in Kansas so will have to come on home after I get on the train…"

Despite these travels and increasing complaints about his health, Theodore remained interested both in the welfare of his Colorado ranch, and in the possibility of acquiring property and mining stocks elsewhere in the

West. In February of 1911, he wrote to his son Gustave: "I hope you will make it all right with your ditch and will come out all right. Get who you can so you can show that we used the water before the Mount Lamborn Ditch Company did." Whether Gus or Theodore secured the aid of an attorney to confirm their water rights is unclear. In any event, other sources kept him apprised of the value of water as, in October of 1914, Merle D. Vincent, an attorney working in Paonia wrote to Theodore asking him: "Will you let me have your check for $470 due on your account?"

The large collection of picture postcards from various parts of the United States that Theodore sent to his son during these years reveal his mixture of interest in his Colorado ranch and his willingness to speculate and invest in properties and mining interests elsewhere, perhaps with the intent of moving to a warmer and drier climate. In February of 1913, Theodore wrote to Gus from Lynn Haven, Florida: "I have sold my lot and the 5 acres for $150.00."

(As evidence of Theodore's far-flung interests, as late as 1924, eight years after his father's death, Gus Roeber still was paying a reduced tax assessment of $120.00 on property his father had bought in Bexar County, Texas.)

Writing from Florida again in February of 1913—this time from St. Petersburg—Theodore was keeping abreast of local doings when he reported that he had managed to secure a Paonia newspaper and noted that, "Ed Sherwood is proving up on some land on Oak Ridge." A stay in Douglas, Arizona, in 1916 found Theodore writing to Gus with a mixed report—on the one hand he declared that "Douglas is not good on account of the smelters" which worsened Theodore's asthma. But, on the other hand, he also informed Gus: "I bought some mining stock, it is copper."

In January of 1914, during his stay in San Antonio, Texas, Theodore informed Gus of his purchase of two lots of land to which his son responded it was "a good inwestment *[investment]*" and added "if you keep on you will have property all over the united states." Gus' approval, however, caused Theodore to write a month later: "I was telling you about my investment. You think it is good, but I sometimes think it is poor. The 2 lots cost 700 dollars that of cours is a good teal *[deal]* of money. I think would have made more if I had invested that much in cattle, would have made better interest. I don't think I am losing anything but will make nothing." Meanwhile, Theodore was pleased to learn, from the bank in Zephyrillis, Florida, that he was receiving 12.5 per cent interest on his dividend of $500.00.

In February of 1913, Theodore admitted to his son, for the first time, that rather than his "asthma," he was instead afflicted with something more: "it is Kidney trouble that is worse... I feel awful weak sometimes." His health seemed to be a growing concern. In one of his surviving notebooks, a penciled recipe for a new concoction of potassium iodide to be taken at every meal suggests that Theodore's breathing difficulties were continuing but that he was trying additional remedies. Perhaps he was experiencing some relief.

The Paonia Booster reported on April 30, 1914, that "Theodore Roeber, well-known pioneer of this end of the county, returned last night from a pleasant winter's sojourn on the Gulf coast of Texas. Mr. Roeber looks as though he had found plenty to eat and had succeeded in shaking off the physical ills which have caused him so much anxiety in the past few years."

By August, however, the newspaper reported that Theodore had gone to Glenwood Springs, Colorado, for a two-week stay. Perhaps he hoped the hot springs there or the caves with heated atmosphere would ease his breathing. He left in December 1914 by train for Florida, the *Booster* concluding that "his many friends are glad to see him improved in health and trust he may find added strength during his winter's sojourn in the south."

However, the June 22, 1916, issue of the Paonia organ *The Newspaper* reported that "Theodore Roeber came in Saturday night from Arizona, where he spent several months. While the trip and change of scene afforded him relief from his physical distress, he is yet not in the best of health." A month later, Theodore was pleased when the same newspaper recorded that his nephew and family, "Mr. and Mrs. Wm. Planner, of Hammond, Indiana, have been visiting several days in the Chas. Vogel home and with other friends in the neighborhood."

In addition to his general health concerns, Theodore had become concerned because the pension he received as a Union army veteran had not reached him. In December of 1913, he wrote to the Department of the Interior's Bureau of Pension noting that he had contacted them in November because he had not received the pension nor "an answer to my letter." He supposed that because the pension had been formerly paid at Hanover, Kansas, perhaps this explained the difficulty. In January 1915, Theodore received a request from the Pension Bureau asking him to update his personal information for the benefit of wife and children. He informed the Bureau of his wife's death in 1901 and gave the names and dates of birth and death of all his children. He had already asked, as far back as 1884, for an increase in the rate of $4.00 a month, citing it as inadequate because of his "Asthma and disease of Lungs." By February of 1916, Theodore received the news from Thomas Duffield, the Vice President of the Fruit Exchange State Bank in Paonia while wintering in Phoenix, Arizona, that his letter "inclosing pension check for $72.00. . .has been placed to your credit as per inclosed deposit slip. . .sorry to hear that you are not feeling well, and believe that when you do come back the bracing air here will make you feel better." By November 1916, Theodore had received a final payment of $24.00 which reflected the monthly pension amount he was to receive during the last year of his life.

With the outbreak of the First World War in August 1914, the cost of living began an increase that was reflected in the worried correspondence which Theodore addressed to several persons. By February of 1915, he was wintering in Saint Petersburg but asking the bank directors in Zephyrillis to mail a "statement of your annual Directors' meeting. Has the Bank paid any dividend?" His son confirmed his father's financial worries in a letter sent to Florida that same month. Taxes on the property had risen considerably: Gus's assessment had risen by $26.00; his brother Adolph's by $14.00; and Louie's by $10.00 and "everybody else is complaining that they are so high and the graising permit is 6 cents higher a head than other years."

In the final four years of his life, Theodore received letters asking for his support of various political issues. C.K. McHarg, the secretary and treasurer of the Bessemer Irrigating Ditch Company in Pueblo begged him to support the state's then-attorney general despite the fact that Fred Farrar was a Democrat. McHarg wrote: "I am a Republican, but I believe that it behooves every man of us, regardless of political faith, to make known to our fellow water users the facts of this matter. To a large extent the success of our pending litigation with Kansas, Wyoming and Nebraska and the threatened litigation with other states may vitally depend upon his renomination by the dominant party." Only Farrar, McHarg maintained, "an irrigation lawyer of recognized reputation" is "fully awake to the State's danger." Farrar alone could fight off the "water pirates" intent on "seeking to devastate our agricultural interests."

The Denver District Attorney Frank C. Goudy, in making his unsuccessful bid to become the Republican gubernatorial candidate, wrote to Theodore hoping that he would "find it possible to assist me. . .if nominated I will make the best fight I know how, and if elected will do my full duty to the people." By 1919, Louis A. Shellenberger would become a settler on the far southern edge of the Roeber ranch but, in 1912, he was the owner of the Montrose-based Colorado Culvert & Flume Company who divided his time between Pueblo and the North Fork. Shellenberger apparently sought Theodore's assistance while organizing the local Bull Moose Party in the doomed attempt to re-elect Theodore Roosevelt President of the United States in 1912. While it does not surprise that Theodore might have been courted by both regular Republican, as well as "Bull Moose" candidates, it is odd that, among his surviving papers, he preserved a circular letter from Woodrow Wilson. That letter highlighted support for Wilson with a plea for the same backing on behalf of Democratic Congressman Oscar Underwood (candidate for President in 1912) because "The Democratic Party is now in fact the only instrument ready to the country's hand by which anything can be accomplished. It is united, as the Republican party is not. . ."

In addition to these political solicitations, a more ominous social-political view which presented local implications loomed on the horizon—one which, by 1917, would engulf Theodore's children. The first hints of trouble appeared in the January 1, 1914, issue of *The Paonian*. The editor, Arthur L. Craig, was an ally and supporter of the Colorado progressive politicians whose Denver leader, George Creel (a close friend of Woodrow Wilson) would eventually, in 1917–18, spearhead a propaganda campaign against the World War I Central Powers—the German Empire, Austria-Hungary, the Ottoman Empire, and Bulgaria. In his 1914 article, Editor Craig lauded the growing population of the town (Paonia) of some 3,000 persons, the quality of fruit harvests, and the contention that "coal of finest quality is mined 2 miles from town & is delivered into bins at an average cost of less than $3.00 a ton." The paper then went on to advertise for more residents. Boasting the absence of saloons in the county, it also declared that the North Fork Valley was *"composed entirely of good American citizens of more than average ability— no colored people, Mongolians, Indians, Mexican peons, nor objectionable races represented."* By 1917, as WW I raged onward, the list of undesirables would include German-speakers.

By the Fall of 1916, Theodore's health worsened sufficiently that he sought more radical medical intervention. Mercy Hospital had opened in Denver in 1901 at 16th and Milwaukee and it was to that institution that Theodore's doctor sent him. It was not for his "asthma" that he would be treated, however, but for a gall stone that was causing him increasing distress. Absent at Thanksgiving, Theodore received postcards from his daughter Mary and her daughter, Dorothy Maria, both wishing him a Happy Thanksgiving and wishing that he could have been home with them for the holiday. Alas, he was destined never to return to the North Fork Valley.

The November 30 issue of Paonia's Democratic Party organ *The Newspaper* gave a front-page story under the headline "Theodore Roeber Passes Away." "As we go to press the sad news comes in that Theodore Roeber passed away Tuesday night in the Mercy Hospital in Denver, after an operation had been made in the hopes of saving his life. The body will probably come in Thursday evening. Mr. Roeber went to Denver several weeks ago to try to get relief from the stomach trouble which has afflicted him for so many years. It is supposed that this is what killed him…he leaves four sons and five daughters to mourn his death. The sorrowing ones have the sympathy of all. The funeral will be held Friday at 2 o'clock p.m. from the Christian Church, conducted by Rev. Wegener." One suspects that despite his own very tenuous connection to the Lutheran church of his ancestors, his daughter Mary, a devoted Lutheran, most likely persuaded the Lutheran pastor Wegener to conduct the funeral. Whether the service was conducted in German or in English, remains unknown. The Reverend A.F. Wegener had begun to hold Lutheran services in German and on every second Sunday in English earlier in 1916, but no evidence survives that Theodore ever attended.

A December 7 life sketch of Theodore correctly recorded his date of birth, but the account already contained inaccuracies—including the claim that he had come to America with both his parents and then enlisted in the 9th Illinois Cavalry in 1861. Contrary to the conclusion about the cause of his death that appeared in the local newspapers, Theodore's surgery for the removal of a gallstone (his daughter-in-law recalled it being the size of a chicken egg), it was pneumonia that ended his life—no doubt due to the chronic weakness of his lungs he had complained of for years.

Theodore's death in November of 1916 was for him, a mercy. Had he lived two more years, he would have had to face the unpleasant outbreak of anti-German hysteria that swept through the country. (That he still remained interested in the place of his birth revealed itself in a clipping from an unidentified English-language newspaper that Theodore kept. Dated "London, Sept. 13," the headline declared: "Kaiser Sends Praise to the Saxon Army.") Also, had he lived a year longer he would have had to mourn the death of his youngest son Louis who would die aboard a transport ship on the way to France, a victim of the Influenza Pandemic. Nor would it have been easy for Theodore to have absorbed the increasingly frustrated ambitions of his chosen successor, his son Gus. Although the future of the ranching operation seemed bright enough when Gus married Fannie Alderson in 1914, the twentieth century would not be kind to that marriage, nor to the ranching aspirations of the couple and their children.

The economic and political struggles that enveloped the family in the United States, however, paled by comparison to the radicalization of their now-distant relatives in Zschopau and Gersdorf with whom they had no contact. By the 1920s, in the face of the devastating economic and social collapse of life in defeated Germany, the Roeber family there would become increasingly radicalized; first as supporters of the Social Democrats, and eventually, the nascent communist movement. As such, more than one member of the family was destined for disastrous confrontation with the radical right-wing movement that came to be known as the National Socialists.

Theodore would never have understood such responses to defeated struggles for economic and social respectability. Throughout life, his own near-fatal descent into abject poverty as a child had continued to drive him toward the hope of a brighter economic and social future. On balance, one can only conclude that—like so many other socially and economically marginal Europeans who shared the same mixture of desperation and hope—he had succeeded, at least in part. The world he left behind for his own children, on the other hand, faced a much more mixed, and fragile future.

Sources

For more on "colonist" or "emigrant" railroad car, see https://en.wikipedia.org/wiki/Colonist-car

North Fork Times Special Edition, 1899.

Paonia and the Upper North Fork Valley: The First 30 Years 1881–1911 (Paonia, CO, 1996).

Delta County Assessor General Land Office Plats.

Theodore and Maria Early Farm File.

Letters and Postcards, Theodore, Gus, Otto, Fannie Roeber 1898–1930

Civil War Pension File.

Medical Recipes, letters File.

Business Papers File.

Theodore Roeber County Assessor File.

Delta County Independent "Know Your Neighbor" undated clipping 1968.

Delta Independent Sept. 24, 1897.

D&RGW Website: https://drgw.net

Stu Carlson, "Historical Highlights: Sam Hartman and the Kings of Cow Country," (October 7, 2020) https://www.highcountryshopper.com/community/spotlight/historical-highlights-sam-hartman-and-the-kings-of0cow-country/article_f7ee8874-08b3-11eb-b3cf77da9dae.html

Chapter Four
Wars, Depression, and Recovery

On December 7, 1916, the same day *The Paonian* presented a "Brief Life Sketch of North Fork Pioneer, Theo. Roeber" the paper on page four announced that "Gus Roeber threshed 225 bushels of fine wheat from three and two-thirds acres of land. If any of our correspondents can beat this record, let them trot it out." Four years earlier, *The Paonia Booster* had announced in January that "Mr. Roeber is hauling lumber for a new house for his ranch." The "Mr. Roeber" in question was Gus, who with the aid of his brothers Frank, Otto, and Louis, along with brother-in-law Charles Wiening, began construction on what was intended to be temporarily a new home. The plan was to build a more permanent ranch house later which meant the temporary log home would become a bunkhouse for a hired hand on the ranch. The logs for the cabin were snaked off the base of Mount Lamborn and built on a foundation of granite rocks that were close at hand. The site was chosen because of those rocks and its unsuitability for cultivation. Once brought down from the base of the mountain, the spruce logs were notched, planed, and squared with a chinking of sand and cement applied between the logs. The roofing was made of cedar shingles. A more capacious and elegant ranch house for the new couple was planned to be built a few yards further to the west of this log cabin structure. Instead, only one "new house" was built, and the "temporary" log cabin would become and remain the home of Gus and his new wife, Fannie Alderson after they had married in Denver on January 21, 1914, and until they divorced in 1945.

As was the case with the generation of Gus' father, the local papers most often noted the activities of the male members of the community and only rarely gave glimpses into the lives of the women of the North Fork Valley. *The Paonian,* apparently unaware of Fannie Alderson's marital plans, did relay some information about the bride-to-be as it reported that same January that "Miss Fannie Alderson, for some time past an efficient employee of the Co-Operative telephone central office, departed on Tuesday of last week for Denver, where she will visit this winter with her sister, Mrs. Claude Fisk." The paper failed to mention that, besides working for the local telephone exchange, Fannie had also been employed as a milliner in one of the Paonia clothing shops. Furthermore, rather than merely *visiting her sister* Stella in Denver, Fannie would ask her to be one of the two witnesses to the January 21st wedding that took place at a Methodist church in Denver. As a result of this wedding, two brothers of the Roeber family—both Frank and now Gus—were married to Alderson sisters. In Gus and Fannie's case, their backgrounds and personalities would prove to be hard to reconcile as they began their married life.

Like the Roeber family, the Alderson family had moved successively from East to West across the continental United States. But the Alderson origins, their ethnic background, and their political and religious views all had little in common with the German-speaking family into which two of Samuel and Mary Caroline Alderson's daughters would marry. Moreover, even the name "Alderson" according to oral family history, did not reveal the actual remote origins of an Irish immigrant family who had arrived in Virginia in the late eighteenth century, with successive moves west through Kentucky, Arkansas, Missouri, and finally, western Colorado.

However, the two families had arrived with decidedly differing documentation regarding their backgrounds. In the case of the Roeber family, the fire that had consumed the original Indiana homestead house also destroyed the bible in which any family records had been kept. In the case of the Alderson family, a very large bible with dates of births, marriages, and deaths survived the many moves across the country and that provides at least some believable data that can be checked against public records. However, just as is the case with the somewhat fanciful tales that became embedded in the migration story of the Roeber family, the same phenomenon occurs in the case of the Alderson family. We can verify reasonably well the persons, places, and some of the events surrounding Fannie Alderson Roeber's parents and grandparents. After that, the remote history, while making for entertaining reading, can be verified only in part from written private and public sources.

One of the earliest Baptist preachers in Virginia, John Alderson, had helped to spread this Protestant denomination's influence in the late eighteenth century through the western counties of that colony (later to become a Commonwealth.) But differences of opinion over Calvinist theology eventually resulted in a split between "Regular" and "Separatist" Baptists. Between 1811 and the 1830s, a movement led by Barton Stone and Alexander Campbell was intent on reforming what they regarded as doubtful doctrine and practice among Baptists. By 1832, this movement gave rise to the "Disciples of Christ." It was this series of events in American Protestantism and this denomination that shaped the later history of the Aldersons as they moved successively from Virginia through Tennessee, Arkansas, and Missouri. Fannie's father, Samuel Alexander Alderson, was born in Madison County, Arkansas, in 1850 and he would marry in December 1871 at Lawrence County, Missouri. His bride was Mary Caroline Risenhoover, herself born in Polk County, Arkansas in 1855. That marriage took place in the home of Mary Caroline's mother, Delilah Risenhoover, who was born in 1838 in Alabama.

It is with Delilah Risenhoover that the more remote history of these families becomes increasingly doubtful. It appears to be true that this woman was born in Alabama, the daughter of James Robinson Kirby (1802–1847) and Cynthia Mayfield (1805–?) and that their history can be traced back to Blount County, Tennessee. But the Kirby-Mayfield history at this point becomes entangled in an oral tale of a claimed connection to the Cherokee Nation, perpetuated by Delilah Risenhoover telling her children and grandchildren that she could not inherit or claim land because her connection to the Cherokee came through her mother, and not her father. Scholarly literature exists which details various wars, not only between European settlers and various Indian Nations in Kentucky and Tennessee, but also between the Cherokee and the Osage and Quapaw in the Arkansas Valley between the 1790s and the 1820s. However, the literature does not reveal any Kirbys, Mayfields, or their marital partners with a connection to the Cherokee Nation. Delilah married successively Asa Risenhoover (1824–55); Franklin D. Cox, and J.H. Pope before she herself died in Salida, Colorado, in 1891.

A similar doubtful oral history claimed that Samuel Alderson was himself the son of an adopted father whose original name was Belew, the sole survivor of an attack that killed the rest of his family while he was absent and in the home of the Alderson family. No records of the various European settler-Indian Nation warfare in Kentucky, Tennessee, or Arkansas confirm the story. That a Belew family did emigrate from Ireland, arrive in Virginia, and settle in Greenbriar County by the 1780s is true. That an Absalom Belew was living in Green County Kentucky in 1800 as was an Aaron Alderson is also true. But their being involved in an Indian massacre cannot be documented.

What can be determined from the Arkansas Census of 1850 is that a William H. Alderson, had been born in 1788 in Kentucky and, at some point, had migrated further west. William's son, Jessie William Alderson, was born in 1820 in Columbia, Adair County, Kentucky, and would die in 1898 in Monett, Missouri. After marrying in 1844 in Benton County, Arkansas, Louvina Williams (who herself had been born in Tennessee in 1826), Jessie Alderson eventually felt himself called to become a preacher. W.B. Cochran of Aurora, Missouri, wrote an introduction to Baptist Theology Exposed and Bandy's or the Preacher's Dream, a book which Jessie Alderson authored. According to Cochran, Alderson had hoped to attend Bethany College. Undeterred by his lack of funds to attend the college, he began preaching on his own among the Disciples of Christ in his home county and in the town of Monett, Missouri, where his attack on Baptist theology was published in 1898.

To Jessie William Alderson's son Samuel and Mary Caroline Risenhoover Alderson, nine children were born between 1872 and 1895, their daughter Fannie being the next to the youngest born in 1892 in Purdy, Missouri. When the Aldersons arrived finally in the North Fork Valley of Delta County, their youngest, Samuel Edwin was born in Delta, Colorado in 1895 and the 1900 Federal Census located all of them in Precinct Five. Samuel A.

Alderson showed as little inclination toward successful farming and ranching as did one of his eventual sons-in-law, Frank Roeber.

In 1905, The Paonia Booster included an advertisement for "The North Fork Realty, Insurance and Investment Co., S.A. Alderson, Manager." Between 1905 and 1916, the Aldersons lived at various addresses and Mary Caroline returned to Missouri with her youngest son to visit relatives. A local Paonia newspaper reported in 1916 that "S.A. Alderson and wife, with their son Sam, Jr. arrived Saturday evening. Mr. Alderson having met the two other members of the family at Grand Junction on their return trip from Missouri. Young Sam seems to have thrived on possum and haws and is almost big enough to lick his dad. Her friends will be glad to know that Mrs. Alderson's health is much better for the sojourn at a lower altitude. The family home is now in the Mortimer Stone cottage on Poplar Avenue."

Why and how Fannie Alderson and Gustave Roeber decided to marry remains a matter of conjecture. That her older widowed sister Mary (Alderson) Allebaugh had married Frank Roeber in 1912 suggests that the two families already knew each other. But an early incident in Fannie's married life, which she later recounted to her grandson, must have given her pause. Wishing to please her husband Gus early in their marriage while he was working with other men in putting up hay for cattle, she took a picnic basket out to him for his lunch. Rather than expressing his appreciation, Gus told her never to do anything like that again because it embarrassed him in front of the other men.

As evidence of Fannie's more lively temper, years later, while her nephew Philip was visiting her on the ranch, Fannie and her sister became so engrossed in conversation that she allowed a loaf of bread to overbake so severely that it came out of the oven hard as a rock. To Philip's astonishment, Fannie dumped the loaf on the floor and proceeded to kick it back and forth with her sister. Philip remembered to his delight her addressing him: "Well, Phil, I'll bet you never knew your Aunt Fan was good at football." In his own declining years, before his death in 1997, Phil Roeber noted the passing of his "aunt Fan" in 1985 and wrote that he grieved to know that yet another of the "bright and vivacious Alderson girls" had died.

Despite her nephew's praises, Fannie was not reticent in making clear her sometimes acerbic observations about the shortcomings of other settlers in the North Fork Valley. Where others referred to the long valley that stretched to the north of the town of Paonia as Minnesota Creek, Fannie referred to the area and by extension, its residents, as "feeble-minded canyon." The incidents and the observations all seem to confirm that Fannie and Gus were not well matched in temperament, background, or expectations of what life on the Colorado ranch would entail.

However, their married life seemed to get off to a good start. In January 1914, even before Gus and Fannie were married on January 21, Gus wrote a letter on January 5 to his father Theodore, who was spending the winter in San Antonio, Texas. The 1914 National Western Stock Show was set for January 19-24 in Denver and, apparently Gus wanted Fannie, who eventually would become Mrs. Roeber, to attend, so—in that pre-marriage letter—Gus informed his father that: "I just got the season ticket for the Stock Show and there is only one that I can use the other one is maid [made] to Adolph Roeber and is not Transferable so its no good to me do you think that you can get me another one in please [place] of it if you can have it mailed to Mrs G.W. Roeber or Mrs Fannie Roeber and mail it to me I think if you wright [write] right away to them and tell them to sent it right away it will get here in time yet. . .hoping that you are well and here from you once more before leve for the show the 18 so I will Close for this time."

Theodore responded on the 12th of the month that he had received Gus's letter and sent his proxies to have Gus vote for him at the annual Stock Show meeting. He also said that Gus should just take the ticket with Adolph Roeber's name on it, inform them that he would not be there and that Mrs. G.W. Roeber was attending in his place. He attached a note to the official in Denver and was sure his son and new wife would be admitted. On February 9th, Gus wrote to his father to say that everything was fine except "old Dewey, he died. We are leving in our new house now and I have a good cook. . .the Stock Show was pretty good this year and had a good time. Fannie used Adolph's ticket she sined Adoloph naim [signed Adolph's name] and their was not thing said she went in on his naim. Well pa pa this is all I know to write for this time so I have to quite [quit]. Your Loving son G.W. Roeber."

Writing later in February 1914, Theodore noted that Gus and Fannie had been able to attend the Stock Show and wrote: "I wish you good luck with your wife." By March, Theodore was in New Braunfels and informed his son: "These is a nice little town, It is a German town you don't hear a word of English here, old and young speack the German language." Theodore's intention of favoring his son Gus revealed itself in his letters and postcards which were routinely addressed to "Dear Son Gust" and usually ended with "Your loving father." A month later, Gus wrote to his father and, after giving him the local news, he added—perhaps tongue-in-cheek: "The news I hear now is that you is married again how about it, are you? I think that someone had dream and thought it was so."

The local paper in Paonia noted that in March "Gus Roeber and wife have made two short visits recently in the home of Mrs. Roeber's sister Mrs. T.C. Fry, near Crawford." As the year drew to a close, another notice appeared announcing that "Mr. and Mrs. Gus Roeber are the parents of a bright baby girl who arrived to claim a place in their home last Thursday evening. Mrs. Roeber who was Miss Fannie Alderson, will receive the congratulations of a large number of friends, as will also the proud father." With Arline Donna's arrival and with Theodore increasingly absent for many months of the year, Gus and Fannie now became the central figures on the German Mesa ranch. Significantly, the name of their eldest daughter and those of her siblings—Charlotte Louella, born in June 1917; Clinton William, born in 1919; and Glenda Elizabeth, born in July 1936—all bore recognizably English and distinctly non-German names.

The July 1916 visit of the William Planer family to the Roeber family and acquaintances in the North Fork Valley, however, reinforced to Fannie Alderson Roeber that she was, in fact, an English-speaking addition to a German family. And she also learned more regarding the internal tensions that existed between Theodore and his sons. While the Planer family was visiting inside Theodore's house along with his children, Fannie was outside working in the garden when her brother-in-law Adolph (Otto) emerged from the house in a bad temper. He stopped long enough to say "it is good that you do not understand German. Father is inside and has nothing good to say about anyone except your husband."

Among the many postcards Theodore sent back to his sons during his visits to various parts of the country, only one survives addressed to Otto. It depicted a burro, and the message read "Dear Son Adolph. I am well hoping you are the same. There are a lot of burros here. I see 4 hitched to the wagon abreast. The Indians know how to use them. A happy new year. Your father Theodore Roeber."

And yet, it was with his new daughter-in-law, who did not speak or read German, that Theodore would sit in the evenings. During these times, he would often darn his own stockings—perhaps having learned this skill from his father Christian, the master stocking-weaver. It was during these evening talks by kerosene lamp that Fannie learned of Theodore's harrowing childhood in Gersdorf, his arrival in America, and his strained relationship with his mother, Bertha.

Despite the outbreak of World War I—announced in bold-face type in the local Paonia papers—the ranch that Theodore and his sons had put together beginning in 1889 continued to prosper during the period from 1914 to January 1917 and the future looked reasonably bright. Although no inventory of the furnishings in Gus and Fannie's new home survives, by 1915 they had purchased a Silvertone record player supplied with Edison needles. The labels on the single-sided shellack 78 rpm records include Pathe, Homestead, Victor, Monarch, Oxford, Okeh, and Columbia records which were shipped by rail as mail-order items from the Sears, Roebuck & Company of Chicago. Since rural electrification would not reach the ranch until the 1940s, the early radio in the home must have been one of several models then available, powered by batteries. Gus and Fannie's children recalled that, by the 1920s, the program their father in particular favored was the Grand Old Opry that had begun broadcasting from its home in Nashville, Tennessee in 1925. In addition to the players and singers on this one-hour broadcast on radio station WSM, Gus Roeber enjoyed the singing of the Carter Family (Sara, husband A.P. and his sister Maybelle) who released in 1927 their first 78 rpm double-sided record featuring some of their most popular songs ranging from folk to gospel, bluegrass, and their own compositions. At some point before the 1920s, the Delta County Co-op Telephone Company expanded from the 90 telephones in operation in the town of Paonia in 1904 to serve rural households including the Roeber ranch.

The increasing prices cattlemen were receiving per hundredweight between 1910 and 1916 (from $4.00 to $7.30) must have encouraged Gus to think that he would be able to realize his father's ambitions of putting together a profitable ranch that now boasted 250 head of cattle and, to secure its future, only needed one or two modest expansions along with adequate water rights for irrigation. Still, two years into his marriage and with a young daughter, Gus did not significantly improve the family's original two-room log house whose only addition amounted to a tar-paper porch/kitchen. Although running water was available in the house, the family would remain dependent on an outdoor privy until 1945; and a wood and coal-burning cookstove in the porch/kitchen and another stove in the living room remained the only sources of heat. Access to the area under the eaves required climbing a steep set of outdoor stairs at the rear of the house, and the shingled roof was not sufficiently snug to prevent the entry of unwelcome insects or the occasional powdering of winter snows. Underneath the house, a root cellar had been dug in order to preserve potatoes, carrots and cabbages buried in earthen tubs with wooden shelves that held canned meats and preserved fruits and vegetables. A smokehouse at the rear of the cabin provided some means of curing pork, beef, or venison. However, the poultry house, pig pens, and corrals for the milk cow and horses lay some 100 yards further to the south and could be reached only by traversing the open fields that lay between them and the cabin.

No graveled or paved roads connected the ranch to the town of Paonia some four miles to the northwest. When Gus or Fannie wished to travel beyond the ranch, either the half mile to the county road where they picked up their mail, or farther to reach the town, this was done on foot, by single horse, by a single-horse buggy, or in a spring wagon if the entire family was to make the journey. By three years into the marriage, whatever plans Gus had for constructing the permanent ranch house and moving out of the "hired hand's" cabin had changed dramatically. With the entry of the United States into World War I in April 1917, the outbreak of anti-German sentiment would complicate the young couple's lives. But that was not the only problem they faced. On January 11, 1917, the Paonia newspaper published a report on "German Mesa" stating that "quite a number of our people have been more or less indisposed with colds, grippe, or threatened pneumonia. Among the worst of these are the Rule family, Skedtstrup's little boy, and Gus Roeber's little girl, but we are glad to report all are better at present." By January 25, the paper reported again that "Mrs. Gus Roeber and little daughter are numbered among the victims of la grippe."

As the Influenza Pandemic spread in three successive waves through various parts of the world between 1917 and 1919, the confident predictions of the Paonia papers about the recovery of the Roeber family proved to be premature. On December 12, 1918, the grim news appeared that "The family of Gus Roeber, whose disease developed into pneumonia, has suffered and Mrs. Roeber was reported Tuesday night to be in a very critical condition, though yesterday brought the good news that she was much better. Otto Roeber and his sister, Mary Sellars, and her daughter are believed victims, all being now reported out of danger."

Three months before this news, bold headlines on October 31, 1918, reported "Hand of Death Falls Heavily Upon Our Community Making Eight Homes Mourn. 'I'll never come back,' said Louis Roeber when he left Paonia on the fifth of August for Camp McArthur, Texas, answering his call to military service. His premonition, it pains us to report, was well founded, for on Monday his brother, Gus Roeber, received an official message which stated that Louis had died of influenza while aboard the transport which was carrying his company to Europe, and that since there was no possibility of returning the body to American soil within a reasonable time, he had been buried at sea, at the next sunrise, with full military honors."

The paper went on to give a brief biographical sketch of the 32-year-old Louis Roeber, noting that he had spent his life on the ranch and as a cattleman. "He inherited a tract of land from his father, the late Theodore Roeber, to which he added a homestead... Paonians will remember Louis as a kind-hearted, industrious young man of the substantial qualities that are sure to achieve success in life." What the papers did not report was the arrival, some weeks after the public announcement of his death, of a postcard from Louis stating, "the ship on which I sailed arrived safely overseas." Written before the ship sailed or during the voyage, the card was not sent back to the United States until after the transport had docked.

Louis' 160 acres that he received from Theodore lay some distance south of the rest of the Roeber ranch and was separated from those properties by a section of un-settled Federal land. It was on this stretch of public land that Louis would in 1915 begin to stake a claim under the revised provisions of the Desert Homesteading Act. Theodore was the one who urged this step because he had become increasingly concerned about the need to acquire land and water rights to lands further to the south of his original purchases. The idea was to fence the combined land off into one working ranch whose care would not be complicated by the need to cross another person's farm. Louis' property included water from land which John Henry Reynolds had homesteaded in 1888 before selling the property to Jacob Miller in 1893. Reynolds Springs provided adequate irrigation for the small farm, retained in a modest reservoir not far from Louis' cabin.

It is not entirely clear why Louis did not continue to make improvements beyond putting up some fence that could still be seen decades later on land that the family commonly referred to as the "Old Claim," but which never became part of the ranch. Under the provisions of the Desert Act, however, had he filed his claim, the chances were good that it would have been accepted. Instead, two years after beginning the homesteading process, Louis moved to the mining town of Bowie further up the North Fork Valley and onto a small farm where he lived with his older sister, Mary, and her daughter Dorothy. With his unexpected death a year later, the task of selling the Bowie farm and purchasing his property on German Mesa fell to his brother, Gus. The effort to make good on the homesteading claim was refused by Federal officials. By the time the filing was attempted, the United States had entered the War against the Central Powers, and it is not unreasonable to speculate that anti-German sentiment played a part in the refusal.

Many years later, Gus confided to his neighbor, Mrs. Julia Trebeck, that he had been reasonably well off until he had to start buying out his siblings. At some point before his death, Louis had begun living with a common law wife, and because beneficiaries had to be named by servicemen before they were sworn to duty, it now fell to Gus to determine how to honor his younger brother's wishes while, at the same time, ensuring that the German Mesa part of Louis' estate would not fall into the ownership of someone outside the Roeber family—a circumstance which would compromise the land and water critical to the ranch's survival. This obligation would contribute, along with collapsing agricultural prices by 1919, to the economic crisis which Gus and Fannie faced by the 1920s. Moreover, by the summer of 1917, the social and political climate in Paonia had turned against anyone with a German name. Although no conclusive proof exists to account for the government's refusal to approve of Gus' attempt to acquire more land via the revised homesteading acts (initiated to connect Louis' property to his own), the general tone of anti-German sentiment that now exploded across the country was evident among Colorado "Progressives" including Woodrow Wilson's Denver ally, George W. Creel. And that bias also enveloped the residents of German Mesa in stories disseminated by the editor of *The Paonian,* Arthur Craig.

On Thursday, July 12, 1917, a banner headline appeared on page one of *The Paonian* that read: "WANTED—NAME FOR ONE MESA, MADE IN AMERICA." The accompanying Editorial went on to claim that a "WAVE OF SENTIMENT Demands Change to More Patriotic Name." Although admitting that "German Mesa" had "developed into one of our largest and most important producing areas, with all branches of the fruit, livestock, and general agricultural businesses" the editor insisted that "we feel safe in assuming that there can be no possible objection on the part of the original settlers, who are today loyal citizens of the United States."

Contrary to the editor's expectations, a letter appeared on August 16 that rejected any name change, pointing to anti-German hysteria elsewhere and that the problem was Prussian militarism, not all things "German." On a more practical level, the letter went on to point out that all kinds of changes in boundary lines and property-related issues would now be necessary—

citing as only one example that "German Creek" was one such critical property marker. Moreover, a recent meeting of a ladies' club resulted in a unanimous vote opposing any change. Arthur Craig's response was to ask "what will people elsewhere think? For us to persist in flaunting 'German' to the world as the popular name of one of our plateaus and streams would be accepted by the world at large as lacking in loyalty, to say the least..."

By January 10, 1918, the demand for a name change took on a more menacing tone. Announcing the "Ultimatum of Delta County 100% American Club," an essay threatened the painting of a yellow cross on the door of anyone suspected of pro-German sympathies. By April the paper announced the creation of the Paonia "Branch of One Hundred Per Cent American Club" with C.T. Vincent, Weldon Hammond, and M.H. Crissman as the governing board, asking that "Reports of disloyal remarks and acts are solicited by the Club. Any case reported will be investigated by a council of five, the personnel of which is unknown even to the membership." Attacks on the speaking or learning German appeared in the following months and, by May 9, W.H. Dean's shoe shop was painted yellow for his failure to sign a Liberty Bond application. The local One Hundred Per Cent Club disavowed knowledge of the act and, on June 13, the paper's front page announced "Yellow Paint Brigade is Ordered to Discontinue" by the mayor of Paonia. By October—ironically only three weeks before the Roeber family received notification of Louis Roeber's death aboard the troop transport, an "Honor Roll of Liberty Bond Buyers" was printed on October 8 that included A.C. and G.W. Roeber, John Vogel, and M.P. Gonner, all German-language settlers on what would now become known as "Lamborn Mesa."

This uglier side of life in Western Colorado did not end with the Armistice. Between 1918 and 1925, the second incarnation of the Ku Klux Klan captured control of the Colorado legislature, the mayor's office in Denver, and the governor's office in the persons of Ben Stapleton and Clarence Morley. The Western Slope branches of the organization were dominated by the Grand Junction editor of *The Daily Sentinel*, Walter Walker. Anti-Black, Hispanic, Catholic, and Jewish speeches and printed materials spread throughout the state during the reign of the Hooded Empire. Until the passage of the Civil Rights legislation of the 1960s, no person of color was allowed to seek overnight accommodation in the town of Paonia. Stung by the anti-German hysteria of 1917-18, Gus Roeber forbade his young son Clinton, born in 1919, to learn or speak German. However, the prohibition did not prevent Clinton's uncle Otto from secretly teaching his nephew a few choice swear words in the language of his ancestors.

Not everyone of some prominence and education on the Western Slope supported the Klan. Robert F. Rockwell, born and educated in New York and with a brief stay at Princeton University, arrived in Paonia in 1907 and began a career as a cattleman and in Colorado politics. Although the Rockwell family maintained a modest but well-built home in Paonia, their main ranch lay outside the North Fork near the town of Maher on Crystal Creek. Rockwell represented the Western Slope in the Colorado House of Representatives from 1915 to 1921 and made an unsuccessful bid to become governor of the State. But this member of the Masonic Lodge and the Rotary Club lost to Clarence Morley, the Klan's favored candidate for the Republican Party.

For Gus Roeber personally, his lack of an education beyond the 6th grade, which was evident in his labored and phonetically awkward German-tinted English writing, extended to his spoken accent. On March 21, 1918, *The Paonian* announced the formation of the North Fork Livestock Association whose Executive Committee included Robert Rockwell and Gus Roeber. Nominated for President of the new association of cattlemen, Gus had refused the nomination because he knew that his German accent was unmistakable, and that in the political and social climate that then dominated American life, he could not represent his fellow stockmen under such conditions. Instead, the President, Vice-President, and Secretary-Treasurer of the new association bore unmistakably English names—Weldon Hammond, D.S. Stephens, and Mrs. Inez Brown. Gus did agree to serve alongside Hammond and Stephens as one of the Executive Committee Gunnison Reserve until 1940. He worked on the Association's advisory board as well.

With the signing of the Armistice on November 11, 1918, the export market for American agricultural products, including beef cattle, shrank drastically. Overall agricultural farm income peaked at 17.7 billion dollars in 1919, falling to 10.5 million by 1921, and by 1932, three years into the Great Depression, had only recovered to the level of 5.3 billion dollars. Cattle prices between 1867 and 1954 increased 230 percent alongside an American increase in population of 330 percent. As farmers and ranchers struggled to adjust to these market conditions, they would not have been pleased to read the analysis of L.D.H. Weld who, writing on behalf of Swift & Co., one of the major packing house concerns in Chicago, published his conclusion that: "Cattle production is becoming adjusted to domestic demand, and will sooner or later bear its nominal relation to other agricultural crops so far as profitableness is concerned." A report in the Denver-based Western Farm Life of May 16, 1923, observed that the shipment of cattle from the American Southwest to the Northeastern markets was expected to be light because there were not enough cattle to supply the growing demand as consumers shifted from pork to beef. Imports from Argentina or veal from Canada were not thought to be significant. Finished steers were at that time bringing in Chicago $10.40 per hundredweight. A surviving 1927 invoice from the C.R. Garner & Co. wholesalers of Amarillo, Texas, detailed the purchase of 20 tons of cattle feed amounting to cottonseed protein nutcake, protein prime meal, and protein prime peacake. The 40,000 pounds were sent, on behalf of the Roeber ranch, to the Fruit Exchange State Bank via freight at the cost of $789.50 with the $286.00 rail freight, at the rate of 71.5, paid by the wholesalers.

For cattlemen in the North Fork Valley, the costs of shipping their cattle by rail also increased significantly. Coal, not cattle, still remained the priority of the Denver & Rio Grande Western Railroad. Cattle from the North Fork Valley were herded onto cars in the neighboring town of Hotchkiss, then shipped over Marshall Pass to Salida where they were unloaded, fed and watered, and then herded back on for the trip to Colorado Springs and eventually, Denver's stockyards. Even with the construction of the Moffat Tunnel in 1928, which eliminated the need for the stop in Salida, the trip lasted a slow 36 hours. Despite the popular description of the "Roaring Twenties," that largely urban prosperity rarely extended to agricultural communities, especially in the mountainous, semi-desert towns and ranches of the Western Slope of Colorado.

By the summer of 1919, Gus and Fannie Roeber were expecting another child. In June, Fannie joined her mother on a trip to southern California to visit her mother's relatives. She sent two postcards with penciled messages, one to her younger brother Samuel Edwin Alderson who had served as a sergeant in the U.S. Cavalry during the War, and the other to her husband Gus. From San Diego, she wrote to her brother: "Dear Bro. how are you, we are all fine. It is hot here and not much doing. There are so many soldiers here they are out of work. Los Angeles is more lively than here. We have seen lots of new things but I wouldn't live here. Mama sends her love to you with mine, Fannie." Her message to her husband was much shorter: "Dear Gus, we are here but we haven't found Aunt Sade or any house yet. Will write in a day or to. We are all well we get along fine. Fannie." After the birth of their son, Clinton William, in October 1919, the family of five spent most of their time working on the ranch and, by 1920, their oldest child Arline began school at the Lamborn Mesa one-room schoolhouse that had been erected on donated land about a mile northwest of the ranch.

By the 1920s, the town of Paonia boasted its own high school that had been built in 1904 but students in the outlying rural districts still had to find their own transport to and from the school. As late as the 1930s, horses and hitching posts and livery stables remained a common sight in the town. Gus' oldest sister, Mary, had moved to Paonia in 1909 and her daughter Dorothy finished her eighth-grade education in the town, and then completed her high school education before earning her bachelor's degree at Western State Teacher's College in Gunnison, Colorado and a later Master's from Iowa State. Beginning her teaching career at the rural Stewart Mesa School, Dorothy rode a horse to and from that school before spending three years in Eckert (Delta County), five years in Collbran (Mesa County), and finally 22 years at the Paonia High School where she taught Spanish, English, and Sociology. Although she attended German Lutheran services with her mother Mary, Dorothy never learned the language of her ancestors. Athletic as a young girl (playing on the women's basketball team at the high school), Dorothy suffered from a condition that caused her to put on weight which she could never control. To her second cousin, she confided in a conversation that she was always grateful to her uncle Gus because he would allow her to check her weight in private by using the large outdoor scales at his ranch where he weighed heavy sacks of grain.

Throughout the 1920s, agricultural prices continued to be disappointing. And yet, in 1928, the town of Paonia opened its first movie theatre, and Gus found the means to purchase the family's first and only automobile. Trying a Packard and several other models, he settled finally on a green and black four door Dodge Victory Six sedan—the last six-cylinder car the Dodge Brothers made before they sold their firm to the emerging Chrysler Corporation. Taking the train to Hartman Brothers automobile franchise in Montrose, Gus had the title made out in Fannie's name at a price of $1,368.00. It would prove to be the only, and last luxury the ranching family would acquire. A year later, in March 1929, Gus made a final purchase of land, acquiring from Louis R. Shallenberger a small parcel that bordered on the south and west of the Roeber ranch with the right to a ditch from Quackenbush Creek to the property. The sum was $10.00 but with the proviso that "no water whatsoever is to be conveyed by this Deed."

By October, the collapse of the stock market brought the entire American economy into the Great Depression; both banks in Paonia would fail. The town's population had already shrunk to 925 by 1920 and would remain in the pre-1910 figures until the worst effects of the Great Depression were lifted by the war economy of the 1940s.

One measure of the Desperation era which Gus Roeber felt over the next three years manifested itself in 1932. For the only time in his life, Gus abandoned the Republican Party of his father and cast his vote for Franklin D. Roosevelt. That he refused to do so again in 1936 reflected in part the failure of the new administration to address the depths of the Depression in the farms and ranches of the American West. The passage of the Taylor Grazing Act of 1934 put an end to homesteading and initiated the pattern of the Federal government granting permits for limited grazing on public lands. This step meant that the Roeber ranch and other members of the North Fork Cattleman's Association had to provide a range rider who would be with the cattle during the summer months to move them from place to place. Such movement was necessary to prevent over-grazing and poisoning of the cattle from whorled milkweed, larkspur, or monks' hood.

Gus and his family remembered all too well their sorrow and embarrassment at being unable to purchase a wool blanket from the once wealthy and powerful cattleman Samuel Hartman (1860–1938.) Hartman had lost his original ranch and cattle in the collapse of prices by the late 1920s. By the 1930s, the man was reduced to making door-to-door visits in the hopes of peddling blankets to make enough money to keep at least his much smaller herd. He ran cattle in the Ragged Mountains at the far northern end of the North Fork Valley. To reach the spot, he travelled from his home in Hotchkiss.

Two years before the 1936 election, drought coupled with the impact of the Depression forced Gus to sell off 75 head of his base herd at a price that had collapsed back to the 1890 level of $2.00 per hundredweight. Some forty years later, after his death, his wife Fannie remarked to her grandson, "Gus just gave up after that."

The dogged loyalty to the Republican Party demonstrated by Theodore Roeber (apart from his support for the "Silver" Republicans in the late 1890s) revealed that he did not support the Montrose, Colorado attorney John C. Bell who won election to the U.S. House of Representatives on the Populist ticket in the late 1890s. During the succeeding Roeber generation Democratic party candidates in Delta County increasingly benefited from the long-standing loyalty of Crawford area residents where many settlers came from Virginia, Arkansas, and Missouri. In addition, the rise of the United Mine Workers in western Colorado during the early 20th century (including the Delta County mining town of Bowie) resulted in the Democrat Edward Taylor representing the district from 1909 to his sudden death in 1941.

Despite his failure to win the Republican nomination for governor in the 1920s, New York-born Robert F. Rockwell won the special 1941 election to succeed Taylor. He served until his defeat at the hands of the conservative Democrat Wayne Aspinall in 1949. Both the senior Rockwell and his son Wilson were acquainted with the Roeber family, largely due to the large Rockwell cattle ranching enterprise and their ownership of a house in Paonia. One assumes that both Gus and his son Clinton supported the senior

Rockwell's political ambitions. Not until the election of 1960 would Clinton Roeber decide to follow his father's example and vote—only once—for a Democratic candidate for the Presidency. By 1980, Clinton Roeber was focused on protection of agricultural lands and smaller coal companies in the face of increased population and service demands. Clinton's disapproval of the Republican failure to promote an adequate plan for economic development which addressed his concerns would lead him to challenge, as an Independent, the Republican County Commissioner Ben Sheldon.

By the mid-1930s, as the economic plight of Gus Roeber's ranch family continued to decline, its composition changed as well. A daughter, Glenda, was born on July 6, 1936, when her mother was 44 years old. On October 29 of the same year, the family's second daughter, nineteen-year-old Charlotte Louella, married the Crawford area sheep rancher Clarence Collins in Delta. Charolette moved to her husband's ranch where the Collins family had been long-time residents of the "Virginia Settlement" in the Upper Clear Fork valley.

At some point during the 1930s, Gus managed to find the money to rent a small house in the town of Paonia so that his children would be able to attend the high school without making the five-mile journey from the ranch. But it was Fannie and the daughters who lived in town; son Clinton rode a horse from the ranch into town, and then back to the ranch to help his father with the cattle and the property. This meant he was unable to join sports teams, devoting what little free time he had to writing and participating in high school dramatics.

As Clinton finished high school in 1938, studying by kerosene lamp since rural electrification would not come to the farms and ranches of the Valley until the 1940s. Upon his son's graduation, his father explained that a basic choice now lay before them: he could sell the ranch, and with the proceeds, he could afford to send Clinton to college as his cousin Dorothy had done. Otherwise, Gus now intended to turn over the running of the ranch to his son. Clinton opted for the ranch even though he had intended—and had been encouraged by his teachers—to attend college.

Clinton's decision triggered his father's own, and by December of 1940, Gus signed over the stock brands he and his brother Louis had received from Theodore; he also started the process of handing over the property of the ranch to his son—a move that would be registered by March 1941. His brother Otto would continue working on his smaller property until 1948 when he also sold his land and cattle to his nephew.

In September of 1939, a petition was signed addressed to the Board of Directors of School District No. 5. Identifying themselves as "legal voters of School District No. 5" the signatories demanded that the district "pay tuition for pupils residing in the district who attend High School in Paonia Colorado, providing satisfactory grades are maintained, and request that you call a special meeting for the purpose of deciding this question." Clinton Roeber's father and mother were not among the signatories.

During the 1930s, the Roeber family acquired new neighbors to their immediate north. Among those signing the petition to the School District Board of Directors were Anton Trebeck (1900–1940) and his wife Julia (1899–1995.) Both of them had emigrated separately from Slovenia while it was still part of the Austro-Hungarian Empire. He temporarily worked in the mining towns of Colorado with the intent of returning to Slovenia. She initially worked in Trieste, the city that became an international protectorate following the Armistice and the collapse of the Habsburg Empire. Unlike the Roeber family, the Trebeck and Urbancic families had not kept extensive records of ancestors, their occupations, or their long-term places of birth and residence. Still, that family had stories to tell and their ultimate connection to the Roeber saga makes their history worth mentioning.

Julia was a descendent of Frank Urbancic, born in 1857, and Mary Fatur, born in 1845, in the village of Knajak. The village lay a few kilometers west and south of the capital (at that time Laibach; today Ljubliana.) The village was situated close to the main road and railroad that ran west from the capital through Pijuca and Postonya in the northwestern part of Slovenia to the coast at Trieste. Seven children born of this marriage survived, five of whom later married and also had children. Julia's father came to the United States and worked in the Pueblo steel smelters twice between 1908 and 1910 before becoming ill, finally returning to Slovenia, and resuming his work in forestry and lumbering. Forestry was as much a way of living as farming in an area whose villages boasted stone houses with tile roofs and interior white plastered walls.

The man whom Julia would eventually marry, told his daughter, Dorothy, about the challenges of working during his early teens. Anton Trebeck said he was expected to work with the men in the grain fields outside the village, wielding a scythe in unison with the others. He explained this meant that, when his nose began to bleed from heat and exertion, he was not permitted to stop to wipe his face lest he interrupt the set-rhythm which the line of harvesters had to maintain to guarantee the successful completion of the harvest.

Anton Trebeck's own father, Jahn, had been a village blacksmith who married Mary Rebec. Both Anton's father and mother were from the village of Klinik, not far from Knajak. Anton's mother, Mary Rebec, had been born in the village of Palcje, and she and Jahn had nine children. Their eldest child, Yvonna, became a nun and died in Ljubliana in 1905. Her younger sister, Maria, married but had no children. The next youngest, Agatha, lived in Fierenzi, Italy, and her younger sister Helena married. Two children, Joseph and Olga also left Slovenia, Olga moving to Rufina, Italy, and Joseph to Paris, France, although he would return to Slovenia in his later years. Of the three remaining daughters, Antonia, Frances, and Katerina, the latter became the stepmother of a daughter, Stanislava, who was then raised by Antonia after Katerina's death. Anton's youngest brother Paul also left Slovenia for Argentina, where he disappeared.

As was the case with many southeastern Europeans who began emigrating to the United States in the 1890s, these people gravitated toward work in the mines and steel mills of states like Pennsylvania, Colorado, and Utah. Many, like Julia's father, never intended to remain in the New World, intent on making enough money to return home and improve their economic and social conditions in familiar surroundings. Anton's own father came to North America in 1910 on the ship *Laura* with his departure town identified as Ostrizsobovo, Austria. Two years later, he made a return trip on the ship

Alice, this time his home identified as Postonja, a town on the main line to Trieste and only a few kilometers from Knajak and Klinik.

His son, Anton, arrived in America in 1923 on the ship *Argentina.* By this time the change in borders that followed the dissolution of the Hasburg Empire identified him as "Antonio Trebec" from the town of Klenek, Italy. It was through his mother's Rebec family that Anton was sponsored for a work permit in America. Decades later, after the deaths of both Anton and Julia, a daughter visiting their home villages made the startling discovery that Anton had a serious love interest in his home village and may not have been planning on staying in America at all. Instead, he and Julia met after both had made their way to the North Fork Valley coal towns of Bowie and Somerset where they both found work. Their courtship was a short one and they were married on April 26, 1924, in the rectory of St. Joseph Catholic Church in Grand Junction, Colorado, by Father Nicholas Bertrand.

These Slovenian laborers in the coal mines of the North Fork avoided the horrors of the Colorado Coal Field Wars of 1912-14 and the infamous Ludlow Massacre of April 20, 1914, near the steel mills of Pueblo, Colorado. Despite the achievements of the United Mine Workers to demand a safer set of working conditions in the coal mines, miners who found work in western Colorado and neighboring Utah still labored under very dangerous conditions. When the Fifth Annual Report of the State Inspector of Coal Mines issued his report in 1917, he noted on page 8 that most of the fatalities suffered were the fault of owners, not the miners, nor even the result of unavoidable accidents.

The 1930 Census located Anton Trebeck, his wife Julia, and their daughter Dorothy living at the far north end of the North Fork Valley in Somerset, Gunnison County, Colorado. But between their marriage in 1924 and the census date, Anton and Julia had moved to Utah to the mining towns of Carbon County: Hiawatha and Sunnyside. Their daughter Dorothy was born in Hiawatha on July 16, 1926, before the family of three moved back to Colorado where Anton found work in Somerset. In 1929, he became a new employee at a the newly opened Bear Coal and Coke Company, taking on roles as a blacksmith and driver of the cars which carried the coal out of the mine. He transferred the coal to conveyors that loaded the coal onto the waiting railroad cars of the Denver & Rio Grande Western Railroad.

Other North Fork residents included the Bear family. They were Croatians who had changed their name (Medved) to its English equivalent. Anton Bear (1899–1959) had himself immigrated to the United States along with other siblings. He married in 1914 and settled in Somerset by 1920. Only three years before, the Fifth Annual Report of the State Inspector of Coal Mines identified only one major mine in Somerset operated by the Utah Fuel Company. But in 1929, the Bear family would open a mine across the North Fork of the Gunnison River opposite the Utah Fuel Company mine and the Denver & Rio Grande Railroad tracks. The mine would prove to be a source of employment, and eventually, grief for the Trebeck family.

Dorothy Trebeck's earliest memories included taking the train from Somerset to the nearby mining town of Bowie to visit Andrew Rebec, her great uncle and his family and to enjoy the wonders of the goods in the general store run by another Slovenian family, the Pavlisicks. She also recalled that a major excitement for herself and the youngsters in Somerset was to watch the steam locomotive move onto the turntable that reversed the engine for the return trip down the valley and onto the mainline at Delta. She was warned that when she took the train to Bowie, in order to reach house and store she would have to walk from the tracks across a bridge over the Fire Mountain Canal and was not to look down into the water lest she lean over and fall in.

In 1929, Julia Trebeck gave birth to a son, Charles. Dorothy remembered her mother boarding the train to take the infant to Delta for visits to the doctor. Despite the devastating impact of the Depression on the agricultural economy, the need for coal by the railroads, steel mills, and other heavy industry kept the mines open and kept Anton Trebeck employed. So frugal was this couple that they were eventually able to pay cash for a farm on Lamborn Mesa when the previous owners defaulted on their mortgage payment. The Trebeck family would move to Lamborn Mesa in December of 1933 while Julia was expecting another child.

Before that move, a tragedy struck the family when two-year-old Charlie developed rheumatic fever and died. As a five-year-old, Dorothy could not understand why her brother would not talk to her as he lay on the bier in the front room of their home in Somerset. No explanation was ever given to her by her parents about her brother's death. The lack of Catholic clergy in the upper settlements of the North Fork resulted in the young child being buried in the graveyard in Somerset under the auspices of the Church of Jesus Christ of Latter-Day Saints. Dorothy attended a Sunday School class provided by the same church.

Sometime during the 1920s, the Trebeck family acquired a monochrome lithograph by William A. Carson (1867–1949) of a shepherd bearing a lamb in his arms. The image was hung on the wall of her parents' home. Young Dorothy concluded that this was a picture of the Good Shepherd she had learned about in Sunday School. Despite the Roman Catholic backgrounds of both the Urbancic and Trebeck families, their oldest surviving child recalled no actual home devotions or other indications of the Catholic faith in the years before her father's death.

Even given the prevailing custom of not smiling when being photographed, Julia's wedding picture and others convey a sad appearance and demeanor. One can perhaps conclude that Julia Trebeck suffered from some form of chronic depression from her earliest years. She seldom smiled, and the death of her son reduced her to hours of weeping while also refusing to comfort her daughter who wanted to be held. Between 1934 and 1940, Anton and Julia would have three more daughters, Jo Ann, born in 1934; Phyllis in 1936; and Lorraine (1941–2020.) Their eldest daughter Dorothy remembered that her father walked the short distance up the road to the home of the Slovenian Kochevar family to use their telephone to call the doctor to come deliver his daughter Jo Ann.

Dorothy was chosen as valedictorian of her eighth-grade class as she graduated in 1940 from the one-room Lamborn Mesa School a half mile walk down the road from her parents' fruit farm. Dorothy's hand-written valedictorian speech called on her classmates to remember "that an education is our most valuable asset, that it is obtained only by hard study, that there is no royal road to success, but an education brings the best reward life can offer. It increases our learning power, it enables us to be leaders rather than followers, it makes us minds rather than machines."

At some point, as she reached her high school years, Dorothy Trebeck began to attract the attention of the young man, Clinton Roeber, seven years her senior and her nearest neighbor. Her own high school studies, however, were to be interrupted a year later just as she began her freshman year; she would not receive her General Education Diploma until decades later.

In September, just as the school year had begun, Anton (Tony) Trebeck was fatally injured at the Bear Mine in Somerset. A blacksmith by trade, a skill he had learned from his father, he worked as a "driver" making sure that the mules were shod and driving the cars these animals pulled in and out of the mine ready to be filled or emptied. Although details of the accident remain unclear, apparently a brake either failed or was intentionally not properly secured on one of these cars, causing it to crash into a second car where Tony was standing. In later years, his widow informed her daughters that she had learned that this was not an "accident" but that Tony was the innocent victim of what was an intended murder of another man—possibly a foreman, or fireboss, or perhaps even a member of the owner's family. That same story was remembered by Bill Wiening, Clinton Roeber's cousin, who had worked in the Bear Mine with Tony. In the Colorado record of mining fatalities, Tony's death was recorded as due to "haulage." Suffering a crushed pelvis, he was taken to the small hospital in Paonia. The extent of his injuries was so extreme that he could not be moved to a larger facility, and he remained bedfast until his death on November 11, 1941, leaving his widow Julia and four daughters on their fruit farm on Lamborn Mesa. Unable to explain to her small daughters why their father was not there, Julia said only that he was not coming home, and later, that he was in heaven.

Although a Catholic parish had been established in the county seat of Delta in 1911, in Paonia between 1921 and 1922, and one in neighboring Hotchkiss in 1923, no priest was resident in each of these small towns. The very first Catholics in the area around Paonia had included the German Mesa settlers Carl Vogel and Mathew Gonner and Bernard Orth's wife, Amelia Koehnke.

Father Emil A. Eckert, born in Bavaria, Germany, came to the United States in 1930 and began his ministry in the North Fork Valley from 1937 to 1945. Although Eckert conducted the funeral for Tony Trebeck, his relationship with the predominantly Slovenian-speaking parish in Paonia was never especially positive. Speaking with a distinct, clipped German accent, Eckert was also an enthusiastic early supporter of the National Socialists, at least in his earliest years in the United States, not unlike many conservative Catholics in Bavaria and elsewhere in Germany. As the U.S. entered the war in 1941 and as German occupation of Yugoslavia had already begun in April 1941, many of the mining families who had originated in the Balkans distanced themselves from the Paonia parish. Tony's wife, Julia, remained a member of the parish, and she did take her daughters to the parish following her husband's death, but she also took consolation over the death of her husband from a Protestant radio broadcast which she listened to on a weekly basis. Just as the Roeber family had no deep ties to fellow Lutherans of the North Fork Valley, the Trebeck family had also not developed a close relationship with the Catholic parish, even after moving closer to Paonia in 1933. The third Trebeck daughter, Phyllis, learned to recite the Lord's Prayer but as an adult revealed that, when she said, "Our Father," she assumed she was praying to Tony.

The rise of the National Socialists in Germany and the subsequent Second World War also revealed how differently the Roeber family in North America had evolved from their now-distant relatives in Zschopau. Although Clinton Roeber was eligible for the draft, when he appeared and took the examination, he was told that he failed and that the examiners believed that he suffered from severe emotional stress and that he would not survive the pressures of combat. Although he never agreed with the board's decision, he did admit that, from his early years to his graduation from high school in 1938, he had constantly prayed that his parents would not divorce, because his mother, Fannie, had begun threatening to leave her husband.

Evidence that the emotional/mental climate in the Roeber household had not been a healthy one manifested itself later when two of Clinton's sisters, both Charlotte and Glenda, developed significant mental health issues that resulted in hospitalization. Unable to serve in the military, Clinton turned his energies to producing cattle and crops to aid the war effort. His neighbor, Dorothy Trebeck, while helping to care for her younger sisters, also wrote regular letters to her cousin Bert De Lost (1916–2012) during his service in the U.S. Army.

By sharp contrast, since the early years of the 20th century, the Roeber relations who remained in Zschopau turned to increasingly radical, pro-socialist political solutions to their economic and social decline. The region was a veritable hot bed of radical ideas. As early as 1903, August Bebel, one of the leading socialists of Germany came to Zschopau and addressed an audience of 5,000 persons—urging them to elect a Social Democratic Party candidate for the national assembly, the Reichstag. The later radical "Spartacist" communist leader Clara Zetkin (1857–1953) had worked in Zschopau as a private teacher for the wealthy spinning factory Bodemer in 1879. This experience deepened her radical convictions which extended to the endorsement of violence against not only property, but also that property's capitalist owners. In 1921, in the aftermath of the collapse of the German Empire, a revolutionary committee of the Communist Party of Germany was organized in Zschopau and both Johannes and Otto Roeber were counted among the first members.

With the rise of the National Socialists and Adolph Hitler's assumption of emergency powers as Chancellor by 1933, both Johannes and Otto were arrested and imprisoned on May 10, 1935. Interned with other political prisoners in the early versions of the concentration camps, at least one of them survived, was liberated, and returned to Zschopau to become a teacher in the local school. The shock of what that Roeber survivor had endured during imprisonment became too much for him to bear, and ten years after the war, he committed suicide. By the late 1980s, when the first American member of the family returned to Zschopau to begin reconstructing the history of those who had emigrated, the ex-prisoner's widow was already too frail and senile to answer questions about what had happened in the town and the extended family. And with her subsequent death shortly thereafter, the Roeber name vanished from the town where it had been a part of its history for at least 400 years.

By 1940, Clinton Roeber's oldest sister, Arline, would leave the ranch and begin working in the County's offices until her July 10, 1941, marriage to Harry Hulteen. The groom was a member of a prosperous fruit-growing family whose orchards lay further to the west of the town of Hotchkiss on Antelope Hill. He and Arline lived in Hotchkiss and Harry began his career as the manager of the North Fork Creamery, making the rounds throughout the county picking up the cans of cream that were left at the roadsides of the farms and ranches for transport back to Hotchkiss.

Shortly after the attack on Pearl Harbor in December 1941 and Adolph Hitler's declaration of war against the United States, Arline Hulteen found herself faced with a renewed anti-German sentiment that threatened her job. She managed to dismiss those suspicions when she pointed to her uncle Louis' name on the Paonia Cedar Hill Cemetery's Honor Roll Memorial of those who had died in World War I in service to the nation.

By 1944, as the Allied victory in the Second World War looked increasingly certain, Clinton Roeber proposed marriage to his eighteen-year-old neighbor, Dorothy Trebeck. Preparations for their marriage on October 15, 1945, included Clinton's being instructed in the Catholic faith and being baptized by Father Emil Eckert. On a more mundane level, preparation for when they would move into the cabin home which Gus and Fannie had occupied since its construction in 1914 included among the top priorities an indoor bathroom. Wartime scarcities nearly cancelled Clinton's hopes but shortly before the wedding was to take place, a small shower stall, sink, and toilet were installed. Clinton's father, Gus, had already laid plans for moving to a new home in the town of Cedaredge, some 30 miles to the southwest of Paonia, at the foot of Grand Mesa. But before he could locate a suitable house, Fannie announced her intention to file for divorce. She did so and took nine-year-old Glenda with her, beginning a life as a cook and manager of apartments moving to various locations in Colorado, Wyoming, and Utah. Although she would visit her son and grandchildren on the ranch periodically, my grandmother never returned to the Upper North Fork Valley. She died in Delta in 1985.

For his part, Gus moved into a small one-room cabin further south of the home he had built on a hill—a spot about 200 yards east of the now-abandoned family home in which he had grown up as a child. Although no longer owner of the Roeber ranch, Gus continued to work with his son for the next nine years. In 1949, he was especially pleased when Clinton had a large reservoir built on the land his uncle Louis had farmed. The Reynolds Reservoir proved to be of critical importance for the next generation of the family in providing irrigation to large sections of the ranch that had previously proven problematic for the raising of hay or other crops. Gus also lived long enough to see the ranch move away from a complete dependence on horsepower when Clinton bought the first tractor. The tractor was a huge "Farmall H" International Harvester that could not only pull a plough, but also wield a harrow, planter, or manure spreader. It was also outfitted with a removable hydraulic system that enabled the driver to lower and raise a multi-toothed hay fork for gathering together windrows of hay and transporting them into stackyards which were strategically located around the ranch fields. The $2,000.00 investment made while Clinton was developing the ranch had secured an essential implement which some regarded as the best-selling row-crop tractor ever manufactured in the U.S. and which remained in service into the 1970s. It was an innovation which put a final end to the use of the "Mormon Derrick" a sturdy crane invented in the nineteenth century by the Church of Jesus Christ of Latter-Day Saints farmers in Utah. That distinctive apparatus had been used by farmers and ranchers in the Rocky Mountain states to raise large shocks of hay onto the stacks assembled at the edges of farm and ranch hayfields.

On Christmas Eve 1953, Gus began vomiting blood and was diagnosed with stomach cancer. He died March 1, 1954, in Hotchkiss at the home of his oldest daughter, Arline Hulteen. Between 1948 and 1956, Gus' siblings—Mary, Clara, Lizzie, and Otto—would also repose, most of them, like Gus himself, on or around their 73rd birthday. In 1952, Julia Trebeck sold her farm on Lamborn Mesa, and with those proceeds, the pension of her husband from the United Mine Workers, and Social Security, she moved to the town of Paonia where she bought a house within walking distance of the Catholic

Church. She lived there with her youngest daughter, Lorraine, her daughters Jo Ann and Phyllis having left Paonia after high school. Eventually, Jo Ann and Phyllis, along with their youngest sibling, Lorraine, all left the area and never returned to the North Fork Valley. In their wake, the repeating cycle of hopeful beginnings, relative economic success, tragedy, and disappointing market conditions which had already manifested themselves in the history of Colorado's Western Slope towns was about to begin once more.

Sources

Claudia King, et al., *Treasured Memories: Paonia and the Upper North Fork Valley the First 30 Years* (Paonia: Paonia Chamber of Commerce, 1996).

Souvenir of the North Fork Valley, Colorado (Reproduction) Delta: The Delta County Independent and Hotchkiss Kiwanis Club, 1973.

Clinton W. Roeber, *West Elk Tales,* 36-39.

Author's copies of newspapers: (originals in Paonia Public Library in 1980s but subsequently lost with the move to the new library).

The Paonia Booster

The North Fork Times Special Edition, August, 1899.

The Paonian

The Newspaper

The Paonia Booster

The Delta County Independent

The Daily Sentinel

Colorado Magazine XV #3 (1938), Wilson M. Rockwell, "The Fruit Utopia of the North Fork of the Gunnison," 89-98.

Marriage Certificate, Gustav W Roeber and Fannie Alderson, Denver, Colorado, 21 January 1914.

State of Colorado *Certificate of Title to a Motor Vehicle,* 11 May, 1928.

The Alderson Family Bible and Alderson File

Trebeck Family File

Letters and Postcards Theodore, Gus, Otto, Fannie, Philip Roeber, 1905–1989.

Arline Hulteen, letters to author, 1978

Stu Carlson, "Historical Highlights: Sam Hartman and the Kings of Cow Country," *High Country Shopper* October 7, 2020.

Robert Alan Goldberg, *Hooded Empire: The KuKluxKlan in Colorado* (Urbana, IL: University of Illinois Press, 1981), Chapter 8.

L.D.H. Weld, *Annals of the American Academy of Political and Social Science,* 89 (May, 1920), 51-54.

James Wayland Bennett, "An Analysis of Beef Cattle Prices," PhD. Thesis Louisiana State University, 1955).

Gilbert Gende, "Market Outlook for Farm and Ranch Products," *Western Farm Life,* Denver, Colorado (May 16, 1923).

H. Lüdemann et al, *Das Mittlere Zschopaugebiet* (Berlin: Akademie Verlag, 1977), 162.

https://www.findagrave.com

https://ancestry.com

Chapter Five

Centennial Celebrations, Partnerships, and Political Ventures

I was born on June 7, 1949, the oldest of three sons and one daughter of Clinton W. and Dorothy T. (Trebeck) Roeber. I was named Anthony after my maternal grandfather and Gregg, as far as I know, only because my parents liked the name. Between 1952 and 1961 my siblings, Denise, Mark, and Chad would complete the family.

This chapter begins in the late 1940s with my own birth and recollections. But it also seeks to document, through public and private sources, the rapidly changing circumstances that have shaped the history of the Roeber family through the turn of the new millennium and the arrival of the fifth generation of family members. The chapter ends with the unexpected and tragic death of Denise Roeber Kossler who fell victim to the Hantavirus in February of 1999 and the on-going consequences that continue to shape the history of the family in the new millennium. The problem of memory becomes especially acute due to the fact that there now existed an 8mm movie camera, which my parents bought in the late 1940s, that has created a record on film. I retrieved those canisters and some years ago had them digitized and copied as "Roeber Family Memories," and the act of viewing those films makes the question of what one *actually remembers* even more challenging.

I don't recall, for example, seeing my mother's sister Jo Ann (Trebeck) Desrosiers at her high school graduation as a three-year old in 1952 and calling out "Jo, Jo"—but she said I did. I do recall being in my grandmother Julia's house on Lamborn Mesa and falling down the stairs there so I must have been no more than four years old since she sold the house in 1953 according to Jo Ann.

My earliest memories that do not depend on film include doing chores with my grandfather Gus Roeber—feeding pigs, chickens, milking cows with him—I had my own small milk pail and stool to go along with his. And I vividly remember walking over to his cabin to visit and taking a hammer along to smash hard pinto beans out on the porch as a favorite pastime. I don't have such a sharp set of early memories of my grandmother, Fannie Alderson Roeber, or my father's youngest sister, Glenda, and they may not have been around much in those first years. I do recall more than one reception at my parent's home with the women in dark dresses, dark shoes, and dark stockings—these were funerals, I suspect—ceremonies for Mary, Dorothy Sellar's mom; for Gus; and for my great uncle Otto Roeber, all of whom died in the early to mid-1950s. I don't recall Gus getting sick on Christmas Eve but do remember visiting him at Arline and Harry's house in Hotchkiss where he stayed until he died—and I have a firm memory of running into that bedroom to see him and not understanding why he wasn't there. He always had some hardtack candy in a jar—a treat which I was allowed to have.

Memories of Gus' brother Otto include him walking down from his cabin in the hills just above our ranch house on the way to town to buy groceries, and his habit of storing his cigarettes in the 1928 Dodge that was parked under the cottonwood trees near the creek. When Otto moved into a cabin in town, my dad and I would visit him and take him groceries. A special treat I got from Otto was a sample of dried figs and the Dutch Gouda cheese—and I still enjoy both all these years later. My father told me that Gus drove the Dodge in which Otto stored his cigarettes until 1948 when he parked it under a cottonwood tree on the ranch and said it was the last time that he would drive it. Years later, in 1967, my classmate and friend Bob Johnson and I started to rehab the car and, when we took the brakes apart, the drums were badly scored—so Gus may have come close to an accident and decided not to drive any longer.

Other childhood memories include my father letting me play with his sizeable Spirit of St Louis model airplane. It had no paint on it—but was quite large—big enough so I actually rode on it when I was very little. I also vividly remember my grandfather having built a paddle wheel toy which sat in the irrigation ditch or creek and as the water turned the wheel it was connected to a man who appeared to be turning the crank that turned the wheel. Not until years later did I discover, on a visit to Zschopau in the *Erzgebirge* in the 1980s, that this was an authentic Saxon child's toy—memory of which must have been passed down from Christian to Theodore to Gus and then to me. I especially regret not having been able to save that toy but of course as a youngster I had no idea of its real significance. At about age six or seven, I was constantly playing Roman soldier. This amounted to dressing up with a cape and aluminum foil over some kind of shield; climbing on my horse, Star, with a homemade lance; and setting off for the "Old House" and other destinations. My dad recognized this and made me for Christmas two swords—one a heavy cutlass affair painted silver with a protective handle and the other a short sword that was a copy of the basic weapon Roman soldiers carried. I played with them for years until they wore out or were broken—and the Roman weapon was made of hickory, so it lasted some time.

While in Saxony during the 1980s, I encountered various Saxon food customs. Upon returning to America, I by chance mentioned to my Grandmother Fannie (Gus's wife) a dessert dish, only to discover that she made something like this for him. It is basically a biscuit dough filled with a custard made of eggs and cream—a memorable dessert which must have been a dish that Gus grew up with in Theodore and Mary's home before his own marriage. But Slovenian dishes also figured in our meals as well—the sweet bread *potica* appearing every Christmas and Easter; the less-tasty *struklji* (a filo-dough filled with cottage cheese and then boiled) during Lent. Polenta and goulash provided a way of using inexpensive cuts of beef, pork, or venison, and if my grandmother Julia discovered that anyone was not feeling well, she insisted on the sovereign remedy--a dram of the plum brandy *slivovica,* guaranteed to burn away all ills. Although home-made sauerkraut was a dish common to both Slovenians and German-speakers, as a youngster I could only muster the courage once to try the blood sausage that in a variety of forms is common to nearly all residents of central, southern, and eastern Europe.

I remember feeding cattle on the sleds and wagons with dad—his building a kind of tent on top of the stacks out of hay to keep the wind off while he loaded—and eventually I got to drive the team with his help. I remember the dances at the Mt. Lamborn Schoolhouse. On those occasions, Otto played violin, and a woman played piano—and everyone did square dances, Schottisches, polkas, two-steps. (After Otto, Mr. John Raber—our neighbor who lived on what has today become the CJ ranch property—played violin for these dances.)

I recall visiting Julia and the Kochevars, another Slovenian family who lived on the corner where our lane met the main county road. I also remember visiting Mrs. Buckley across the road and the Arlie Rich family further up toward Dry Gulch on what had been the Haley place. Mr. Rich did the haying for us, using a horse-drawn mower, and the family had a large fire bell attached to a pole in their yard—which they only rang for meals—ringing at any other time would have signaled a fire. I recall that Mr. Rich's son and I got into trouble because we trashed Otto's cigarettes in the parked 1928 Dodge and I think it was he—a boy some years older than I—who helped me dismantle my father's brick forge—provoking dad to be angry and call me a "little Vandal"—to which I apparently replied, "tell me just one thing—what is a Vandal?" He reportedly found my question very funny.

In the same shed containing the forge, a box with a hinged lid held tools. But one summer it contained a nest of bumblebees—I lifted the lid and let it slam as they started swarming—and one of them stung Gus on the nose—I don't recall if I was stung or not.

I do recall being ill with mumps, measles, and chicken pox, lying in my parents' bed next to the front wall of the house, and banging on the wall to stir up wasps or yellow jackets that had made a nest between the logs and chinking. Wasps were a constant plague, and I recall being stung in my bed on more than one occasion.

Remembering Reputation and Prosperity   147

Early ranch dogs included Jiggs and a remarkably talented cow dog named Lucky who, however, had a bad habit of teaching younger dogs how to get into the hen house and suck eggs. He was also very interested in the remnants of the cream cans we set out for collection and once managed to get his head stuck in the can after which he careened around, banging into the house until we rescued him. Neither dogs nor cats were allowed in the house during my childhood until I was in the seventh grade when my mother relented and allowed a new part-Siamese kitten to become a house cat—a house cat who nonetheless spent a great deal of time outside accompanying me on irrigating errands, feeding hay to the cattle, and tending to other chores.

I was very allergic to grain dust and, when our neighbor, Emil Damon, came with his combine to harvest wheat or barley, I was at the granary as dusty sacks were being unloaded whereupon I started having an attack of bronchitis or some other shortness of breath. I was also very allergic to alfalfa hay and working in it with my dad caused severe outbreaks of itching along my legs—sometimes I would scratch until the skin was quite raw. I recall having a viral infection of my upper airway during the night as a child and having my mom take me into the bathroom and turn on the hot water in the shower to create steam to get the breathing under control. The diagnosis was croup—the same affliction which was especially bad for my sister, Denise, and my youngest brother, Chad.

My memories of my childhood house include especially the stove in the living room that had to be heated with coal or wood and a similar one in the kitchen—and running from the shower/bathroom through the kitchen into the living room to be near the stove to keep warm—and backing into it once and burning myself. The basement was accessed from the outside—a cellar door on an incline that was lifted up to reach steps going down to the place where canned fruits and vegetables were kept on shelves. The basement also contained a milk/cream separator that was used after we brought milk from the corrals. The separated cream was placed in cream cans for pickup by Harry Hulteen, my uncle, who ran the North Fork Creamery in Hotchkiss. The remaining skim milk was carried to the pens to be fed to the pig, along with whatever vegetables or other consumables weren't used in the house.

When the house was expanded in the mid-1950s, the cellar itself was dug out to accommodate a coal-burning furnace and a coal bunker. The bunker was filled from the outside by my dad bringing in a pickup load of coal. As I got older, my job was to make sure that the "clinkers" (that is, waste lumps of incompletely burned coal) were prized out of the periphery of the furnace. I was also responsible for making certain there was sufficient coal shoveled into a worm-drive stoker because, if insufficient coal reached the furnace, it started smoking and filled the whole house with fumes. I recall forgetting to do this on occasion and being rousted out of bed by my dad to go down and correct the oversight.

The telephone service throughout the 1950s remained the old Cooperative line with the telephone on the wall and where the length and number of rings informed one of whether someone was calling us—or someone else on the "party line." Long distance calls could only be taken by driving into Paonia to the Bell Telephone exchange.

Stories from my mother's childhood included an incident she told me about her being outside while her mother, Julia Trebeck, did the wash. My mother Dorothy, was playing with a kitten with a string, backing up, and accidentally falling into scalding water which left permanent scars on her abdomen and side.

It was my mother who had learned to play basic pieces on the piano which a cousin, Dorothy Sellars, had given my parents and my mother responded to my request to take lessons on an instrument I continue to play even now more than half a century later. My father had learned to "chord" as an accompaniment to his uncle Otto's violin playing, and he could also use a harmonica, which he learned to play from Otto. By the time I was in junior high school, I also learned to play the cornet, although never with great facility. Oddly enough, my favorite 78-rpm record as a very young child was a recording of Enrico Caruso singing "La donna e mobile" from Verdi's opera *Rigoletto*. I played this vintage recording so often that the center hole of the record eventually became unusually enlarged so that the disc itself was no longer stable.

By the time I had reached junior high school, I discovered the early "folk song" groups such as the Kingston Trio and Peter, Paul, & Mary. I also discovered recordings of the musicals: *Oklahoma, My Fair Lady, The Sound of Music,* and *South Pacific.* The comedian/satirist Alan Sherman's rendition of "A Letter from Camp" prompted me to buy that record. Sherman's record, like other recordings by the early 1960s, were never available in the old 78-rpm format. Instead, that format was replaced by the new 33 (technically 33 1/3)-rpm long-playing, double-sided records. A new stereophonic record player—a much appreciated Christmas present for the entire family—was acquired to accommodate the new formats.

However, our new stereo did not entirely replace listening to radio broadcasts of "The Jack Benny Show," "Amos n' Andy," and "The Great Gildersleeve." Television remained a special treat, which had to be experienced in a former neighbors' home in Delta where I can recall seeing the Brooklyn Dodgers play the New York Yankees for the World Series in 1956. By the late 1950s a visit to my grandmother Julia's house in town also included permission to watch an occasional program on CBS, the only network available in the North Fork at that time.

I cannot recall my sister Denise's birth in October 1952 as such but there must have been some anxiety issues early on because dad and mom later told me what happened when mom was gone to the Delta Memorial Hospital for the birth. At that time, my grandmother Julia came to look after me in my parents' absence and I informed her that, if anything bad happened to my mom, I didn't want to know. I must have been easily frightened as a child since folks sometimes laughed about my habit of grabbing my head and ducking down—especially when we went to the movie theatre in Paonia, and the MGM Lion would roar.

I do have quite vivid memories of sitting on fence rails in the evening with my aunt Phyllis and singing songs—I recall "A Song of Love is a Sad Song" from what I remember as the *Hi Lilly* movie (starring Leslie Caron) so that must have been around 1953—and I would have been four or five.

At some point of time, when I was first introduced to my aunt Phyllis' fiancé, Floréncio Daniel Valdez, I apparently reacted in a way that revealed views about Spanish-speakers which I had picked up as a child. Mercifully, I don't recall the incident but have been credibly informed that my response was: "You don't mean you're going to marry a dirty Mexican?" Since in later years my Spanish became fluent, I carried on many a conversation with my uncle "Dan" and he was always gracious enough not to remind me of my bigoted childhood comment.

My aunt Jo Ann had graduated high school and left for college in Grand Junction, so I had less contact with her than with her younger sister, Phyllis. I do remember being introduced to Jo Ann's fiancé, Paul Desrosiers and his family in Grand Junction, and I remember their wedding at St. Joseph's Church where I served as ring-bearer. My mother's youngest sister, Lorraine, lived in town with her mother and consequently, I also had less contact with her growing up. My father's oldest sister, my aunt Arline, visited the ranch fairly often, mostly just to walk in the hills, visit places she remembered growing up there, and spend time identifying flowers and plants.

Arline's husband, Harry, also came to our place regularly from Hotchkiss, but his trips usually focused on hunting jackrabbits of which there were a very large number given the absence in our area of any significant predators. The other nuisance vermin he hunted—and I did too in the course of time—were the many prairie dogs that infested the hay fields as they expanded their troublesome "towns." Skunks were present too and they threatened the chickens on the ranch and occasionally tangled with the ranch dogs, as did porcupines—with meant time spent extracting quills from faces and bathing dogs in tomato juice, then keeping them at a distance for days.

In the skies, Great Horned Owls were common in those days because there were no eagles—certainly no Bald Eagles and large Golden Eagles were very rare and tended to stay at elevations higher than our ranch. Red-tailed hawks and sparrow hawks were more common sights among the raptor population. Robins, meadow larks, magpies, red-winged blackbirds, and mourning doves were frequent visitors and, very rarely, a Baltimore Oriel would appear. In the early 1960s, a successful re-introduction of wild turkeys nearly failed because of the increasing number of coyotes in the foothills. Garden snakes, Bull snakes, and a generous population of frogs could be found on the ranch along with bottom-feeders like suckers that inhabited reservoirs and the North Fork River itself and eventually, rainbow trout, which were successfully stocked by the 1960s in streams and reservoirs.

Dad and mom bought a green Oldsmobile, probably in late 1949 or perhaps the early 1950s—I don't recall travelling in dad's pickup truck but probably did—and got carsick going down Turkey Creek Canyon which was the way one got to Denver over Monarch Pass and Colorado 285 north. Even though McClure Pass had been opened in 1924, connecting the North Fork Valley to Redstone, Carbondale, and Glenwood Springs, it was an *unpaved* road and only used during summer months. The connection between Glenwood Springs, Interstate-70, and the Eisenhower Tunnel to Denver only became possible in the late 1960s. Trips from our ranch were primarily to Paonia where, during the 1950s, a broad range of stores still provided nearly everything we needed. A Safeway store opened on the main street, creating a second grocery store in town. The town had both a men's and women's clothing store along with the First National Bank, Howard's Cash Hardware, and the D.C. Hawkins Insurance Agency.

These stores lined the main street alongside Allison and Dale's Implement and Garage which handled large farm equipment repairs. Tom Polous' movie theatre included not only the showing of "shorts" before the main feature but also, from time to time, a modest lottery based on ticket stubs for which the winning prize was one dollar. A fairly small but for me, very important town library opened up an avenue for reading, a passion that has stayed with me all my life. Until it burned in 1989, the Odd Fellows' Hall remained a gathering place for wedding receptions, and meetings. For me, the Masonic Hall remained the mysterious place, off-limits for Catholics, of course. But the post-World War II years witnessed the growth of both the Rotary Club and the Lion's Club. Clint Roeber became a charter member of the latter at the time of its founding after World War II.

We made more extensive trips, beyond the Upper North Fork, to the county seat at Delta, rarely to Montrose, and even more rarely all the way to Grand Junction except at Christmas time for shopping. It was on a shopping adventure to Grand Junction that I first saw the electric trains I loved. I initially had a very simple circular track and perhaps two or three cars—Marx products—similar to the Marx toys which my dad had in his childhood. His vintage Marx items included a black-faced minstrel with a violin made out of tin and a policeman seated in a car whose head turned right and left as the wheels of the car turned. I recall shopping for shoes in Delta at (I think) Renfrow's, a process that included having your feet put into a machine that X-rayed them—everything looked green—probably an unhealthy practice, but part of the fascination with atomic energy in those days.

The yearly holiday routine was pretty much always Christmas Eve with Julia; Christmas Day was at home and just the immediate family; New Year's Day with the Hulteen family in Hotchkiss—my aunt Arline favored an oyster stuffing in the turkey which I never liked as I also never liked venison, liver and onions, or any kind of fish. Thanksgiving was spent with Clarence and Charlotte Collins and their children in Crawford—a pretty dismal affair since Charlotte was suffering from chronic depression and mental health issues. Easter was again at home; a non-church ritual included picking bluebells along the creek and bringing a bouquet to mom on May Day. When I got to school the May Day celebration included a May Fete—which meant going to the town park and dancing around a Maypole.

Church was at Sacred Heart— and the priest Father McGrath—an Irishman, with his mother living with him in the rectory. The rectory next to the small church was one of the simple mining town cottages—porch, living room, kitchen, and bedroom. Of course, services were in Latin and Father McGrath insisted on wearing his cassock all the time and he also angered the Protestant town by insisting that, as a priest, he should have free water, electricity, and fuel. He was not very popular with the men of the parish—Slovenian males either stayed at the back of the church or waited outside or didn't come at all. After Mass, women, including Julia Trebeck, her sister Mary, and their neighbors would talk in Slovenian on the church steps after Mass, a practice still in use in the mid-1960s when Julia's sister Anna arrived for a visit from Tripoli, returning to her village in Slovenia before her death.

Vacation Catechism School was conducted by visiting nuns from Denver or other places—usually for a week right after school let out. When asked, in first grade or about that time, what I intended to be when I grew up, I apparently indicated that my plans for the future were to become pope. I recall hearing the news of Pius XII's death and the election of John XXIII and I also remember an earlier visit in our area from the formidable Bishop Joseph Wilking of the Diocese of Pueblo. The bishop was on hand for confirmation. He was a dour looking type who put fear into the *confirmands*. Thankfully, when my turn for confirmation came, I was relieved to discover that the new bishop, Charles Buswell, turned out to be a much warmer and pastoral man than Bishop Wilking.

As for other encounters with religious leaders, I have a very positive recollection of a visiting Franciscan—Father Conrad Loftus—who at that time was connected to the Lowry Air Force Base in Denver. Father Loftus came to our area for a brief summer visit which must have taken place during Father McGrath's vacation. Fr. Loftus was a young man who, from time to time, rather than wearing sandals, sported cowboy boots under his Franciscan habit. I recall giving him a big hug and, when he departed, missing him—because he was a warm and sympathetic priest. Another churchman who impressed me was Father Hickey whose stories of his own early priesthood fascinated me because he had lived through the Blitz in London during World War II, and he remarked that he had seen many a bomb fall.

In 1961, with the arrival of Father John Martin as priest, the atmosphere of the parish church changed, and on the whole, I think, for the better. Fr. Martin had grown up as a Methodist, was an electrical engineer by training, and was a late convert and seminarian who had been ordained after attending St. Thomas Seminary in Denver in May 1951. He earned the respect of the men of the parish by doing a lot of repairs and physical work himself. He also began a custom of sponsoring a men's luncheon at the rectory, and organized hiking and swimming trips for the boy altar servers in the parish. He was also diligent in visiting the homes of everyone in the parish on a regular schedule. On a personal level, he encouraged my interest in reading about the history of the Church and the liturgical changes that began occurring in the early 1960s as a result of the convening of the Second Vatican Council. Prior to his arrival, it is fair to say that anti-Catholic sentiment in the North Fork Valley was still very real. I recall vividly the hostility that John F. Kennedy's candidacy aroused among some of my schoolmates and their families and being questioned rather belligerently by one irate Protestant woman after the election about who my parents had voted for. Father Martin's behavior, his joining the local Rotary Club, and cultivating positive relationships with still-suspicious Protestants marked a significant change in the Catholic parish's standing in the larger community.

Ranch duties in the 1950s were my father's alone except for hiring a "hay crew" during the summer months. But from Spring through Fall, dad would have to walk the Beaver Dam ditch from the head at Smith Fork down to Sam's Divide where he left his pickup truck. I recall watching with my mom for his headlights far off in the distance as he came over Sam's Divide at night which meant he was on his way home for supper. Besides the tractor and the pickup, however, haying was still done initially with horse-drawn mowers and a dump rake, the latter of which I learned to use at age 12—which meant learning to catch the team of horses and put on their harnesses and the "Boston hitch" which was the way we hitched them to the double-trees front and rear of the sled or wagon or hay rake they were pulling.

Although an old manure spreader and a drill or harrow were left from horse-drawn days, by the 1950s my dad was using the tractor to plow, harrow, and plant—although he did broadcast seed as well. Besides alfalfa for hay, he also sowed oats. By the early 1960s, he began planting corn which was harvested for sileage for the cattle. I learned to irrigate with him at a fairly young age and would walk with him to learn how to turn the water out of headers into the furrows and then be sure the water got all the way to the bottom of the fields. The corn presented a real problem because it was grown on the field directly to the south of the "Old House" on a steep pitch. In the mornings, despite my best efforts, often enough I'd find that the water had jumped several furrows. The errant flow was cutting a large path through the corn on an angle and heading for the lowest part of the fields and down into "the Oaks"—an area full of oak brush which lay directly to our south and bordered on Bill and Tiny Wiening's place. Dad was also especially worried about poisonous and invasive weeds. So, cutting out prickly burdock, going after Canada thistle, and pulling up milkweed all played a role in various chores I recall doing.

My closest neighbor and friend, Chuck Bear, lived in the house my grandmother had sold to his family—that sale took place when I was about four years old. We spent lots of time playing either "Civil War" or "Cowboys and Indians." This amounted to dressing up and taking off into the hills above the ranch where there were large granite boulders which we designated as "Indian Rocks." Several tragic events which occurred during the early 1960s remain fixed in memory, the first of which devastated Chuck's family. The day before Thanksgiving in 1962, I was already in bed when the phone rang, and I heard my folks' startled and strained voices. I came downstairs and they informed me that they had just been told that Margaret Bear, Chuck's mother, had been killed in a car crash on the highway near Aztec, New Mexico. Charlie, Chuck's father, was badly injured, and Chuck was hurt as well but not as seriously. I served as an altar boy for Margaret's funeral, and I recall having Chuck stay overnight with us for a while after the accident as his father recovered.

Tragedy also visited another of my friends. Just one year earlier, during my sixth-grade year, I had become increasingly close to my classmate, Mike McMillan. We often called each other by phone in the evening to compare homework assignment results. The McMillans also ran cattle, although not on our range, and Mike often enough wore western-style shirts and boots to school. In 1961, his dad, Bill McMillan, died suddenly and unexpectedly, and Mike was absent from school for a week or so. I struggled to find the words to express my sorrow at the loss of his father.

The last of these tragedies occurred when a group of high school students were involved in a fatal car crash at a notorious four-way intersection near the Stewart Mesa Schoolhouse. One of the young men survived the crash, but his heart was irreparably damaged. Fr. Martin managed to give him the Last Rites of the Church and I ended up serving at a funeral that was attended by the local high school students and faculty—one of the few times when the small Catholic church was filled beyond capacity.

Besides these extraordinary events which hit close to home, as an altar boy I was routinely pulled out of school during the week to serve at funerals at Sacred Heart. These funeral duties were in addition to routine rotations among the altar boys which meant I was periodically taken to town for a 7:00 a.m. Mass, after which I walked quickly to my grandmother's house for a fast breakfast, then had to make the final trek to the junior high school before the first bell sounded.

When not tapped to serve at morning mass, going to school meant catching the bus on the main road a half mile from our house. I often walked alone to that stop—or a bit further to get on the bus with Chuck Bear. I followed this pattern until my sister, Denise, started school and we walked together to the bus stop. Different teachers in different years created warmer memories of some, less so for others. Mary Childress made my first-grade year a positive one, and I didn't realize until later that she was part of the Crawford-area families who had been ranching in that community. In my sixth-grade year, Mrs. Florence Wetterick decided that her pupils needed to learn the "Palmer Method" of cursive writing, although I never became much of a penman. Nina Den Beste helped to improve my tortured relationship to mathematics, and Calvin Campbell, a contemporary of my father, encouraged my already-developed interest in history. In Mary Boland's English class in the eighth grade, I discovered the joys of Gilbert and Sullivan's music and lyrics—a discovery which has remained a source of delight ever since.

In late 1955, I lined up with all the rest of the school to receive the first injections against polio. That injection was uneventful, unlike my earlier experience with the first variety of penicillin that I had received for a throat infection. The early version of the antibiotic was a thick, viscous liquid that easily plugged the hypodermic needle. I still recall the nurse, Margaret Patton, being very apologetic as she was forced to insert the needle repeatedly before she got the job done.

Although I was a merely passable student athlete, my seventh and eighth grade coach, James Wilson, was quite disappointed when he learned that I would not be playing football for Paonia High School but was instead leaving the North Fork Valley to attend school in Ohio. I had broken my right arm as a ten-year old, and I also broke the ring finger on my right hand while playing football during my eighth-grade year.

In March 1966, one of the faculty fixtures of education in the North Fork retired. My father's cousin, Dorothy Sellars, had taught at a number of Western Slope schools starting in the 1920s. In 1944, she began teaching Spanish and English at Paonia High School. Active at both the state level and in the National Education Association, she was a frequent visitor to the ranch, and one of the co-authors—along with her cousin and my father's oldest sister, Arline (Roeber) Hulteen—of the typescript family history which I mentioned in my Introduction and again in Chapter Two.

I recall only a few incidents where I got into serious trouble. I managed to behave at school until my eighth-grade year when a number of us boys were grounded during recess for throwing snowballs at the side of the gymnasium. On the ranch itself, I remember being told not to eat the dog food pellets after watching our cow dog Lucky enjoying them—but I did so anyway and got a very cursory swat from my father. But neither he nor my mother gave out physical punishments—their disapproval was sobering enough. I also capitulated once to Chuck Bear's suggestion that we take a swim in one of the stock ponds on the ranch. I did so even though my father had forbidden this for fear that we might drown—a fate that did in fact claim the lives of more than one youngster during the years I was growing up. The worst disobedience I was guilty of—an indiscretion which could have led to real disaster—occurred when I explained to my younger sister Denise that the "cheat grass" which grew up around the hay yards was very dangerous because it could catch fire during a lightning strike. To illustrate my point, I struck a match to a patch of the grass only to be horrified at how rapidly the experiment turned into a blazing inferno in the hay yard. That near disaster brought my parents running from the house to our rescue—and resulted in my being sent to bed without any supper.

When I was in grade school and junior high, my "career" choice was pretty much already fixed and more realistic. No longer harboring an ambition to become a bishop or pope, I was content with the idea of becoming a Catholic priest and serving somewhere in Colorado. I did fill out a form in my high school freshman course for Paonia High and indicated that Notre Dame was the university I expected to attend. In part that choice was dictated by a series of yearly hunting visits by a family friend, William "Curly" Kerr from Denver—visits which began in 1956 and continued for many years thereafter. Curly had attended Notre Dame himself, and I recall that his background influenced my expectation.

As my plans to enter the priesthood continued to develop, I remember attending our eighth-grade dance at Paonia Junior High (in the building that had, until the 1960s, been the original high school) and filling out a dance card, getting a boutonniere for my jacket from a greenhouse on Lamborn Mesa, and enjoying the dance. I was already planning to go to a minor seminary for high school and at first, my choice was to attend the high school in Oklahoma City—where our then-bishop Charles Buswell had resided before he became Bishop of Pueblo. But I was surprised when our then-pastor Father John Martin showed up at the house for dinner to inform my folks and me that the bishop wanted me to go to the Pontifical College Josephinum in Worthington, Ohio, an academically demanding school for serious students where I had been awarded a scholarship at the bishop's request.

It was only later that I learned I had scored unusually high on the standard tests that were given to students. Commenting on my accomplishment, Fr Martin told me: "You must have eaten your oatmeal that morning." At any rate, I had no idea where Worthington, Ohio, was. Moreover, the prospect of going all the way to Ohio was rather daunting but, of course, it was exciting as well. In order to afford the cost of travel, the tuition, and other things needed, I had to undertake some additional chores during my 8th grade year. And locating burdock, chopping it out, and administering weed poison was the most unpleasant chore that I can recall. I remember finding extensive patches of it growing under the oak brush near some of the hay fields and I probably only did a moderately decent job of eradicating it.

The need to irrigate, mow, and then stack hay for feeding the cattle included erecting deer fence around the haystacks. These stacks were located at various points at the edges of the fields and where uncultivated hills full of sage brush, oak brush, and junipers gave excellent cover to deer herds and also large numbers of jack rabbits. Deer had been scarce and presented few problems to ranchers and farmers during the 1930s and into the early 1950s. But by mid-decade they had increased in population and at times the large bucks would get their antlers tangled in the fence and sometimes die there. A surviving photograph in the December 27, 1956, *Denver Post* showed my father extricating one of these victims from our haystack yard with the note that "deer have already ruined six tons of hay at Rober's west slope ranch." A few years later, that newspaper also ran an entire colored magazine insert with photographs by Monk Tyson that highlighted the ranch and other cattle operations on the Western Slope, including very small operations of only a few head as well as larger ranches. By the time my father had consolidated his holdings in the mid-1950s, the ranch consisted of 1,162 acres of farmed and grazing lands and a herd of some 300 head of cattle.

Although I learned how to irrigate, fix fences, and work with my father in the hay, I was much happier riding for cattle, especially when this included moving the herds of the North Fork Cattlemen's Association over Minnesota Pass and into the high-country public lands where they grazed during the summer. My first visit to the "cow camp" at the head of Smith Fork occurred in 1956 when my father took me with him to spend a few days helping the range boss, his cousin Bill Wiening. Our task was to keep the cattle moving to various parts of the range. A later visit to the area with both my mother and sister included going fishing on Coal Creek. The area where we fished must have been fairly steep and the water depth and velocity significant because I fell into the creek and was caught in a whirlpool that kept me underwater until my father managed to rescue me.

My closest companion in those early years was my sister, Denise. She very gamely accompanied me on the knight-errant battles, and when I decided to dress up and pretend to be a priest, she was my altar server. That she was my constant playmate was no surprise since Denise and I were the family's only two children in that first decade of living on the ranch until my two younger brothers were born in 1959 and 1961, respectively.

My younger brother Mark was born in January 1959, and I became very attached to him. When I spent a week at the cow camp later that year, Bill

Wiening noticed that I was rather quiet and not very happy. He asked what the problem was, and I acknowledged that I missed my baby brother. Two years later, my brother Chad was born, and the most vivid memory I have of that event was my aunt Jo Ann calling our house from her home in Grand Junction. In response to her observation, "I hear you have somebody new in your house," I replied, "Yes, I have a new kitten," a reply that positively failed to impress her. Given the ten and twelve-year differences in our ages, I did not have the same relationship to these youngest members of the family that I had with my sister until much later in our adult years. My youngest brother Chad maintained from his earliest years a quiet and deliberate demeanor and it took something extraordinary to get him excited. I was working outside near the house when he came to get me at a very leisurely, strolling pace to announce: "Mark's in an emergency." When I ran to see the nature of the "emergency," I found my brother had, while playing, fallen into a large patch of cactus. And he was not happy with the laconic pace at which his younger brother had gone for help.

I left home at the age of 14 to begin high school in Ohio. For a teenager who was excited about an adventure, I was oblivious to the impact which my departure had on my parents and younger sister. My departures each Fall were much harder on them than I realized at the time. Only years later did I discover that my dad cried every Fall when I left—of course, he did not show that level of sorrow in my presence. When our priest announced to the parish that I was leaving for seminary, I was a bit taken aback to see how little enthusiasm there was among the parishioners when they heard the news. That lack of enthusiasm may have resulted from a misunderstanding. I was told later that some parishioners suspected I was being sent away to school for some kind of misbehavior.

My parents took me to Delta in September 1963, where I caught the Trailways bus for Pueblo at the "Delta House." Arriving in Pueblo, I met a fellow seminarian, Jim Skotnicki, and he and I then boarded a Denver & Rio Grande Western train to Denver where we transferred to the California Zephyr that took us to Chicago. Jim's Polish American relatives lived in Chicago, so we were met at Union Station, and we visited his relatives before going back to the station to catch a Pennsylvania Railroad train east to Columbus.

The Zephyr was an elegant train, but the "Pennsy" Railroad by 1963, was running a number of pretty run-down and uncomfortable trains. The overnight journey meant that, as the sun rose in Ohio, I was stunned to see it as an orange ball on the horizon—so completely unlike the sunrise I was used to viewing in the thin air of the Rocky Mountains.

As I settled into Ohio, I could hardly believe how humid and oppressive the climate was—including the stickiness of the bannisters on stairways in the buildings. There were no phone calls home, but an obligatory Sunday night letter was to be written to parents with the envelope left unsealed so that the Disciplinarian of the High School could read each letter before it was mailed. Other than going home for Christmas, the entire year was spent on campus. There were supervised hikes to neighboring small towns occasionally and "visitors' days" that brought parents of students who lived nearby but left those of us from a far distance on our own—unless we were invited to join the visiting families for a dinner.

Like all other Americans of my age and older, I can recall exactly where I was when, on November 22, 1963, a classmate rushed into the study hall and yelled out that President Kennedy had been assassinated. The seminary cancelled classes and prayers for the dead were immediately said by all faculty and students, followed days later by a requiem mass for the first Roman Catholic to have been elected President.

The town and county grew in numbers by 1950 to some 1,200 persons and it is that size town and its schools, shops, and buildings I remember. The "stagflation" of the 1970s would eventually undercut the post-World War II prosperity, a pattern temporarily halted by the boom in the coal industry that increased the town's population by 1980 to over 1,400 persons, a level that has remained more or less constant into the first decades of the 21st century. The once-booming fruit industry has been replaced gradually by a combination of organic farms, vineyards, and wineries. Increasingly, many who have moved into the North Fork Valley work remotely, a luxury made possible by the erection of towers capable of providing internet and cell-phone access—though admittedly reliable only in some locations. But these arrivals and their work have failed to provide a tax base to replace the vanished fruit farms, coal mines, and hard-pressed livestock operations.

The place I grew up in during the 1950s—and left behind in 1963—had changed significantly from its pre-World War II conditions and Kennedy's assassination and the foreign policy decisions made by his successors would alter it even more. A new generation of people had arrived in the North Fork Valley. Some new arrivals were veterans who had benefited from the GI Bill and obtained a college degree and with that degree, access to jobs in education, retail store management, or working for the Forest Service or Bureau of Land Management.

Some of the pre-War dimensions of the Western Slope persisted; the mining of coal remained vitally important for the local economy. This was so, even though the vast amounts of coal mined in Somerset, the Hawk's Nest, and Oliver mines produced tax revenue for *Gunnison, not Delta County*. Fruit production remained very important into the 1960s and orchards still covered both the mesas and the Valley floor. Many women in the North Fork area went to work in the packing houses during the fruit harvest season. Small farms that boasted a small collection of cows, pigs, sheep, poultry, and horses continued as before, but would, by the mid-1950s, face increasingly poor market conditions—limitations which would cause their gradual disappearance in the next decade. Although horses were still in use on various farms and ranches in the early 1950s, they became increasingly scarce, replaced by tractors, hay bailers, combines, and sleds. By the 1960s, the arrival of the snowmobile provided another way of getting around the ranch to feed cattle or to check on the stock during calving season.

Politically, the county retained its regional colorations—the Crawford area still resolutely committed to the Democratic Party, a reflection of the original southern states from which many of the residents had come. The City of Delta retained mixed affiliations, with Cedaredge and the upper valley towns of Hotchkiss and Paonia leaning more toward the Republicans. The mining families of Bowie, and those who worked in Somerset, but chose to live closer to Paonia, were predictably UAW members and conservative

Democrats. (The UAW, typically abbreviated United Auto Workers, is fully named the "International Union, United Automobile, Aerospace and Agricultural Implement Workers of America" and its membership encompasses a wide range of workers.) The last Western-slope governor I recall was Dan Thornton, a Gunnison-area cattleman who like the Roebers at that time, raised Herefords. U.S. Representative Wayne Aspinall, a conservative Democrat, dominated the entire post-war decades until the late 1960s. On the local level, the former banker and Crawford town leader, Leslie Savage, would play a major role in pushing through various bills in Congress that would create new sources of electric power to the region. I recall visiting him in his home in Crawford with my father and listening to his distinct "southern drawl." At the time, I had little sense of how important a role Savage had played in creating the Crawford Dam and Fruitland Mesa water projects.

By the late 1950s, growing awareness of the inadequate approach to the growing and marketing of cattle led my father Clinton Roeber to begin exploring additional sources of income. He became a licensed outfitter. From the late 1950s until about 1970, he routinely helped hunters find, shoot, and then pack out deer and elk from the hills of our ranch and out from the higher elevations in the Gunnison National Forest that border the ranch. He also began investigating the new technology and approach to the artificial insemination of cows in order to produce leaner and larger cattle for market. To that end, he enrolled in a course of study in Woodstock, Illinois and, by 1964, he was a licensed artificial inseminator for the region, representing Armour & Company.

Moreover, his concerns about needing a more efficient way to make a living as a cattleman coincided with his conviction regarding environmental policies. He believed that such policies being pursued by government at the local, state, and Federal levels were not adequate to deal with what he saw as a looming crisis. For someone who had not been able to pursue a college education, he read incessantly on these concerns and on a wide variety of other subjects.

One of my most vivid memories came when my father announced his alarm and delight in having read Rachel Carson's book, *Silent Spring*. This

1962 exposé of the devastation of animal life caused by the widespread and indiscriminate spraying of DDT informed his life-long search for ways of controlling invasive and in some cases, poisonous plants both on the ranch and in the surrounding private and public lands.

The later 1960s and early 1970s would prove to be even more challenging for the Roeber family as well as the surrounding community as national economic policies and the international conflict of the War in Southeast Asia took their toll. From a purely local standpoint, a kind of "high point" of prosperity and profile had occurred in the very late 1950s. In 1959, the Paonia High School football team won the state championship for its division and enjoyed another winning season in 1961. Chase Wiening was the quarterback for this latter achievement and the entire town turned out to greet the returning bus and the triumphant team. Beneath the appearance of prosperity, however, more ominous signs were already becoming apparent, although few recognized them at the time.

By examining the *Colorado Agricultural Statistics* for the years 1949 to 1960, one can discern the larger patterns that became more acutely obvious at the local level during the 1960s. The April 1961 final statistics for 1959 and preliminary findings for 1960 reveal that cash farm income in Colorado derived from livestock and products rose from the 1940s to 1951. Between 1955 and 1957 that income declined and, by 1959–60, recovered but only back to 1950 levels. Beef cattle prices per hundredweight peaked in 1958 and declined thereafter. The publication of the Colorado Crop and Livestock Reporting Service concluded that the "average value per head for all cattle January 1, 1961, was $135.00 compared to $131.00 January 1, 1960, and $158.00 two years earlier." In analyzing fruit harvests and shipments, the report focused on Delta and Mesa counties for the period 1949–1960. This focus revealed that, whereas more than 40 carloads of peaches were shipped by rail and truck at the beginning of the 1950s, total shipments had declined to around 25 a decade later.

Ranching and farming, anywhere in the world have always been at the mercy of unpredictable weather. The drought conditions of the 1930s that had led Gus Roeber to being forced to sell off most of his base herd did not return at that level of severity in the North Fork Valley until 1977. Moreover, in addition to a dependency on water for irrigation and stock, both fruit farmers and those engaged in raising livestock faced periodic late Spring freezes that could bring economic ruin for the year.

During my high school years, even though I returned from Ohio to work every summer on the ranch, I did not witness in person some of the challenges those years from 1963 to 1967 brought with them. My father hosted an open house at the ranch in the Spring of 1964 to exhibit the first calves born as a result of his pioneering artificial insemination program. A year later, however, I did experience a devastating example of how unpredictable weather could undercut what should have been an economic success story. Returning from Ohio in early June 1965, I learned from my father that a very late freeze had occurred. The oak brush that is quite thick on most of the mesas in the North Fork Valley had already produced the first leaves of the season when unexpected freezing temperatures killed the leaves. After thawing, this interruption in the growing cycle meant the leaves remained a tender and inviting crop for cattle who were grazing in the foothills. Every morning, my father and I would saddle horses and ride out to discover yet another carcass of our herd that had fallen victim to poison contained in the frozen oak brush.

By 1965, as the United States became more involved in the War in Southeast Asia, the impact of that conflict made itself felt indirectly on the air quality in the North Fork Valley. In order to supply wooden pallets needed to transport ammunition and machines, large sawmills were opened at the lower end of the Valley near Delta. In addition to sawing the lumber, however, the sawdust, shavings, and un-used wood were burned in large amounts. The resulting smoke moved up the North Fork Valley and created an impaction that kept the polluted air trapped along the Valley floor but at times expanding even up onto the surrounding mesas. Natural gas would not come to the North Fork Valley for some time yet and most homes continued to burn coal and wood as the source of heating. All these particulates had a noticeable impact on the valley's air quality.

The issue of the Vietnam War became increasingly personal for me by the late 1960s. During my long hours spent reading in the Wehrle Memorial

Library on the Josephinum campus, I became acquainted with the magazine *Ramparts*—a Catholic publication that was politically very left-leaning and an early and harsh critic of the War in Vietnam. *Ramparts* published deeply satirical cartoons that lampooned Francis Cardinal Spellman of New York—a vocal supporter of Lyndon Johnson's increasing commitments to the war. In addition, the magazine also published first-hand accounts of veterans who described the torture of suspected Vietnamese insurgents.

Although my status as a student in a seminary gave me a draft classification of IV-D (4-D), I became increasingly convinced that the Vietnam conflict failed any test of the definition of a "just war" which I knew Catholic theologians had developed. I took a leave of absence from the seminary in 1969. Then, instead of accepting my bishop's invitation to finish college and pursue graduate theological study at his own alma mater, the Catholic University and seminar at Louvain, Belgium, I gave up my IV-D status and registered as a conscientious objector. This meant I had to defend a dossier of arguments I had compiled from various Catholic theologians and bishops. My request to be classified as a conscientious objector might well have failed had it not been for the argument advanced in my support by one member of the review board. During my summers at home working on the ranch, I also helped to organize and direct a children's choir that sang during the annual Fourth of July "Cherry Days" festival in Paonia. This board member was so impressed by that volunteer work that he made it clear he would not vote to send me into combat and possible death.

A near contemporary from Paonia was not so fortunate. Dan Rockwell had graduated from Paonia High School a year after my class. I knew him only slightly but knew a good deal about his father and grandfather. The awarding of the "Rockwell Cup" for academic and overall student excellence was a yearly event at Paonia High School. When Dan was faced with being drafted, he and his family took a step which I myself had contemplated if my request for conscientious objector status were to be denied. In 1970, the Rockwell family left the United States for British Columbia. Dan grew up there and remained in Canada until 2007 when he returned to bring his terminally ill father Wilson back to the Crawford-Maher community. Wilson died that same year, and Dan remained in that region until his own death in 2022. With their departures, another dimension of the history of the North Fork Valley—a dimension which had existed since the early 1900s—came to a close. I witnessed that change in my own family.

Even though my father maintained his life-long loyalty to the Republican Party, he became increasingly critical not only of candidates like Richard Nixon, but of tendencies within his own contemporaries in rural and small-town America. By 1970, he resigned his membership in the National Rifle Association, observing to me that it had ceased to be an organization of people interested in hunting and the responsible use of firearms. In his judgment, it was now a lobbying group for arms manufacturers who were determined to ignore the growing instances of gun-based violence in which weapons were being used that had nothing to do with hunting and recreation.

The summer of 1969 proved to be the last one in which I was deeply involved with the ranch and the larger community. Accepted at the University of Denver's Lamont School of Music, I had already secured as a kind of preliminary positive judgment from the piano faculty at the Ohio State University. Those music educators had listened to and approved of a tape of selections which I intended to send to Denver as part of my application.

As with my previous schooling, my summer months were spent on the ranch working with my father. One memorable project was constructing a flume for the Beaver Dam Ditch across a large gulley. That same summer the North Fork Cattlemen's Association also constructed a new building to house saddles, bridles, panniers and other equipment which the riders at the Smith Fork cow camp needed. I helped complete that task during the month of June 1969 and, by August, I assisted in moving the herd on a long drive which would turn out to be my last. By September, I had started university in Denver and, in order to meet all the requirements—which included preparing sophomore, junior, and senior recitals—I did not return to the ranch during the summer months.

By 1973, the full impact of the oil embargo of that year, and the "stagflation" in the American economy that had first appeared in 1970, combined to produce long lines of cars hoping to buy gasoline during the first of a series of subsequent energy crises. During this period, the 1974 *Colorado Agricultural Statistics* noted that "despite the higher cash receipts, realized net income per farm in Colorado dropped 19 percent to $6,971 per farm...the cost of production increased sharply, particularly for the livestock industry." (p. 92)

Addressing, in part, this 1970s' period of turmoil, Clinton Roeber's recollections were compiled by his grandchildren, John, Kris, and Kelsey Kossler. In *West Elk Tales II: The Creation of a Wilderness*, he wrote: "In the winter of 1974–75, I was forced to sell cattle at below cost prices, and it was apparent that I would join the great number of cattlemen that were going broke if I did not find another source of income. My friend Bill Bear offered to give me a job in the Bear Mine, and I accepted. While I worked in the mine, my daughter Denise and her husband Steve Kossler, took over the management of our cattle ranch. Two of our sons, Mark and Chad, worked when they were not in school." (p. 36)

In April 1977, as a record drought gripped the area, the Holly Sugar Factory that had opened in Delta in 1920 closed. This closure forced many producers to sell or to convert their lands to the cultivation of corn for livestock consumption. These changes, in turn, flooded the market, driving down prices for that commodity as well.

Clint Roeber's summary of events also revealed what now became a new, and established pattern in the family and the running of the ranch. An outside source of income would prove to be critical from the 1970s onward and securing that outside source became a necessary component of the lives of the next generation—beginning with Steven and Denise Kossler, and only a few years thereafter, Mark and Johanne (Vervloet) Roeber. It also demonstrated that the ranch could no longer be run by one, lone operator/owner. If one looks back at the attempts to do just that, the pattern is clear.

Theodore Roeber began the acquisition of land in 1889 but, by 1906, he had effectively turned over the operation of the ranch to his sons, especially Gus. Although Theodore remained interested in the ranch until his death in 1916, he had functioned as the main owner/operator for only about 16 years. Gus Roeber assumed control of the ranch with his father's death but, a year later, he had to acquire his younger brother Louis' property in the settlement with Louis' common-law wife. Gus effectively ran the operation alone for 25 years between 1917 and 1942. My father, Clinton, assumed ownership of the ranch in that year, and managed it for 32 years between 1942 and 1974. By the mid-1970s, the challenge that faced the family was how to sustain multiple families required to operate a ranch which was failing to produce sufficient income to support more than one owner/operator.

With my own departure from working even part-time on the ranch, a good deal of the work with both the cattle and upkeep of the ranch itself fell to my younger sister, Denise. Possessed of an uncommon rapport with horses, she had entered county rodeo competitions during her high school and college years, as well as excelling in music and academic subjects in high school, winning the Rockwell Cup in her senior year (1971).

Eventually, a new set of family members would emerge to help sustain the ranch. In 1969, Galen and Norma Kossler moved to the North Fork Valley, leaving behind a ranching operation in the Boulder, Colorado, area that had begun in the 1860s. Josef Kossler (or Kößler) had been born in about 1840 in the Tyrol, Austria. Eventually, he married Maria Kresenz Drechsel (1847–1932.) This family was probably connected to the Josef Kossler born in 1826 whose wife was Kreszentia Thoeni—and the names Joseph and Kreszenz have continued to be used in the family.

After the Galen Kossler family arrived in North Fork, one of the sons, Steven, took a serious interest in Denise Roeber and the two began dating. They continued seeing each other during Denise's college years at the University of Northern Colorado in Greeley. Married in August 1974, Steven and Denise moved into what had been the Kochevar home where the present-day Roeber Road meets the main county road. Steve assumed many of the duties Clint Roeber had been forced to abandon and he also began working in the Bear Coal Mine. Throughout her own life, Denise taught school, opened a daycare center in their home, and worked additional jobs to supplement the modest income the ranch could provide.

By 1979, my brother, Mark Roeber, returned from the Colorado State University to work and live on the ranch. He and Jody Vervloet were married in January 1981. Jody's father, Willem, had worked all over the world for Dutch Royal Shell. Willem married Elaine (Schreck) Mattison, herself a descendant both of German Catholics and the Protestant Madisons of Virginia. Jody's addition to the family brought income into the ranch operation as a licensed nurse, but envisioning how this next generation would be able to continue ranching required some imaginative re-structuring of the operation.

After retiring from his work in the mine in 1980, Clinton Roeber decided to run for the office of County Commissioner. He first challenged Ben Sheldon in the Republican primary, and because he came close to winning that challenge, he decided to run against both Sheldon and the Democratic Party candidate as an Independent. Explaining his main concerns in an interview printed in the *Paonia-Herald* in August 1980, Clinton criticized the lack of adequate planning in the face of expected population growth, with some special attention paid to the question of whether smaller coal companies would be able to continue to compete against larger, strip-mining companies in other parts of the country. In a more extensive interview in the Grand Junction publication *The Daily Sentinel*, Clinton repeated the themes he had voiced as a member of the Delta County Planning Commission. A more imaginative plan was needed, he argued, to promote farming and ranching, newer and more diverse industries, small coal company operations, and protect wildlife habitat. Although unsuccessful in his bid to become County Commissioner, my father maintained his interest in these issues for the rest of his life. Fully involved in his community, he also pressed for a more modern, larger, and competitive combined Paonia-Hotchkiss high school—goals that would not be realized until more than a decade after his death in 2005.

In 1980, the first steps were taken that changed the nature of the Roeber ranching operation as it had existed since the 1890s. In a series of meetings with the Nature Conservancy in Denver and the Town of Paonia, the foothills above the hayfields of the ranch became part of a wildlife protection zone. This area was permanently barred from later development, even in the event that the ranch as a whole was to be sold. At the same time, the Town of Paonia was to be allowed to build a large water storage facility on a parcel of land given to the town by the ranch. That parcel was given in exchange for the town's agreement to lay a covered pipeline to replace the Beaver Dam

Ditch—a more modern pipeline extending from its source down to the first of the Roeber reservoirs. A second stage of the agreement was to follow, with a pipeline to replace the so-called "extension ditch" from the first reservoir to the larger Reynolds Reservoir completed in 1949. Although the construction of the storage tank and the first pipeline were completed, forty years later, the second agreed-upon laying of the additional pipeline has never been completed.

Internally, the ranch was also, as of 1980, transformed into Mount Lamborn Ranches, a Limited Partnership. Although Clinton and Dorothy were now formally retired, they held shares in the partnership and were to be paid a yearly income while Steve Kossler and Mark Roeber were designated the general partners in charge of running the ranch affairs. Both Chad Roeber and I held fewer shares in the partnership and as limited partners were not involved in the ranch operations. For the balance of that decade, the new partnership arrangement increased the volume of irrigation water to the ranch, secured the foothills against development, and enabled the fourth generation of family members a plausible way to continue ranching.

Five years into the new decade, my parents celebrated their 50th Wedding Anniversary with a dance and reception held at the VFW Post just outside Paonia. Both Mark and Chad Roeber were now married. Chad had married Jennifer Blair. Her father, Jack, was proprietor of the D.C. Hawkins Insurance Agency, the oldest surviving company in Paonia, and her mother Mary is a devoted gardener and housewife. After finishing his DVM degree, Chad had joined a practice in California, returning to Colorado a year later but not settling in the North Fork Valley.

By the 1990s, the ranch had also been increasingly governed by holistic grazing practices in which grazing cattle are moved frequently in order to minimize any damage to a particular part of a range, private or public. In 1993, Mark Roeber wrote to me that "we have a coalition formed between local government, business interests, and 'environmentals' to pay for an economic study and draw a plan to help influence federal agency policy towards county economies. . . .closer to home, our pool got the o.k. to begin the process of managing our allotment holistically. The first step is to have public meetings to draw everybody's viewpoint and then to form a goal. Other than the fact of more meetings, we are pretty excited."

The West Elk Grazing Allotment was finally founded to include six families who all agreed to use this approach. By the mid-1990s, the Allotment won an award from the Society for Range Management and a year later it was honored with the National Range Management Award. For a time, it appeared that a long-range alliance might be formed between the older families who were involved in raising livestock, and newer arrivals in the Valley who became increasingly concerned about unplanned development and the impact this would have on the quality of life both for humans and the native flora and fauna. Bumper stickers appeared, proclaiming a preference for "Cows, not Condos."

As the need for pasture and production of a hay crop became more acute, the cattle were pastured during the winter months on rented ground near Delta. Closer to the home ranch, the CJ ranch, acquired by one of the major national coal companies, provided another source of hay for winter feed with the ranch buying the rights to irrigate and harvest the hay crop. A brief flurry of activity appeared to threaten this arrangement as the coal company considered selling the land for more housing development. A sober analysis of the lack of sufficient water to provide taps for any future housing put an end to those plans.

In a further attempt to make a broader and newer public aware of the ranching operations in the Valley, a coalition of six ranching families also put together what became known as "Homestead Meats." From the locally grown cattle, each of the ranches contributed to the market. Processing and sale started first in Paonia, then expanded to a plant in Cedaredge and eventually, Delta. Other meats besides beef were added to the items for sale. As a public relations gesture and as a means of providing employment for those who worked in the processing and sale of the meats, the venture garnered support not only locally, but from purchasers in other parts of Colorado, and eventually, from mail-order customers as well.

During the 1980s, my family and I had lived for two years in what was still a divided Germany. In addition to conducting research for academic publication, I also used the years there (during a period which allowed visits into East Germany) to secure documents that began a reconstruction of the Roeber family history in Europe and the initial migration to North America. By 1988, after returning from another year in Berlin, I suggested assembling the results of my research into the family history to date as part of a planned centennial celebration on the ranch to be held over the Fourth of July Cherry Days in Paonia in 1989. Invitations went out to all of the near and more distant relatives related to Theodore and Maria Roeber. The celebrations at the ranch featured materials recovered from archives in Germany and North America, as well as articles of clothing and other memorabilia that had survived the 100 years of the family's residence on the ranch. The celebration was held first on the ranch and then expanded with a float drawn by a team of horses driven by Clint Roeber for the annual Cherry Days parade.

Sadly, Arline (Roeber) Hulteen—who, along with her cousin, Dorothy Sellars, had done so much to document the family history—had died of cancer in 1985 before the celebration took place. Fannie (Alderson) Roeber had also died in 1985, leaving only Julia Trebeck as one of the last survivors of the previous generation who was present at the centennial celebrations. Both Julia Trebeck and Clinton's sister, Charlotte Collins, died Julia in 1994 and Charlotte in 1995. Both had lived long and full lives, but no one in the family, indeed no one in the surrounding community, had any reason to expect that a case of what had been known as "Four Corners' Disease" would occur in Delta County in February 1999.

Although the Hantavirus is carried by various rodents in the American West, in Colorado it is spread through the aerosolized urine of the deer mouse. Since documented cases had occurred in the low-lying areas around the far southwest corner of Colorado, no one had any reason to expect a case to strike a ranch that lies some 6,000 feet above sea level. First recognized and identified in 1993, the virus had been responsible for 16 cases and 10 deaths in Colorado in the previous six years. Unexplained cases of severe disease and death among the Utes, and among European settlers discovered in remote cabins point to the long history of the virus' unsuspected presence. And yet, because there had been no documented instances of the virus in

Delta County or the surrounding area, doctors who were called on to treat Denise Kossler believed at first that she was suffering from a severe case of influenza or pneumonia. Before she could be airlifted from Grand Junction's St. Mary's Hospital for treatment at the University of New Mexico—which, at the time, had the only extracorporeal membrane oxygenation machine—my sister died.

After his wife's death, Steve Kossler was left to manage both the household and the ranching responsibilities as well. Of his three children, only his eldest daughter, Krysenz (Kossler) Allen, would return to the North Fork Valley after completing her college education and beginning a career as a teacher in the Delta County schools.

My brother, Mark Roeber's oldest son Chase, after graduating college in 2008, would also be the only one of Mark and Jody's children to return to the ranch to assume increasing responsibilities. This became especially the case after Mark successfully ran for the office of County Commissioner in 2012, becoming the first of the Roeber family since Theodore's lifetime to hold an elected public office. In 2024 he also agreed to run as a candidate for the Republican Party's bid for the District 58 seat in the Colorado House of Representatives. He lost the primary bid by three votes.

Clinton and Dorothy Roeber would outlive their daughter, Denise, by six and 18 years, respectively. But Clint had already begun showing signs of the onset of Parkinson's Disease that eventually took his life. The third-generation couple lived long enough to see the marriages of some of their grandchildren and the birth of the first of their great-grandchildren.

Born in the first two decades of the new century, the fifth generation of the modern-day extended Roeber family with their children has faced one of the most severe and long-lasting droughts on record. This reality has renewed the necessity to adapt in order to manage a modestly profitable ranching business while remaining engaged in the conservation of land, flora, and fauna that had emerged by the 1960s as a matter of deep concern to their great-grandfather Clinton. They do so in the face of a national polarization that threatens the capacity of local and regional communities to find common ground and shared goals on which they can work together. While these patterns are discernible everywhere in the nation, they especially threaten communities that have never been characterized by stable income and strong local institutions. This family has managed to survive over five generations of frustrated ambitions, unexpected tragedies, and fleeting years of prosperity. Such challenges, along with climate and weather, promise to shape their future in the twenty-first century and will continue to dictate whether and how they will endure. Their German-speaking, Slovenian, Dutch, and Scots Irish ancestors were compelled to emigrate, and to re-locate more than once in America. So far, however, their descendants, like the Ute Nation that had been displaced before their arrival in western Colorado, can also say after five generations spanning 135 years, "we are still here."

Sources

The "We are still here" motto has been used both in a film about the First People of Australia, but also at the University of Texas at Austin's Indigenous People's Day since 2015: https://liberalarts.utexas.edu/nais/news/indigenous-peoples-day-at-ut-austin/

Colorado Agricultural Statistics, Floyd K. Reed, et al., Colorado Crop and Livestock Reporting Service (Denver, 1961); and for 1973-74.

Letter of J. Mark Roeber to author, November 7, 1993.

Copy, Selective Service System Student Certificate, August 7, 1967.

Ohio State University School of Music letter to author, May 16, 1969.

Clinton Roeber, *West Elk Tales II* (private printing).

Newspaper clippings:

The Paonian, Nov. 28, 1962; March 24, 1966.

The North Fork Times, September 4, 1980; August 16, 1980; October 16, 1980; October 30, 198.0

The Delta County Independent, April 28, 1955; January 1989; March 28, 2007.

The Paonia Herald, August 14, 1980.

The Denver Post, December 27, 1956.

Afterword

This book has used the device of tracing the history of a patronymic, that is, the last name of the male head of a family, from what historians call the "early modern" era of the late sixteenth century to the present day. By using the surviving local records located in today's Germany, the book documents the fortunes of a family that for centuries enjoyed some reputation and modest prosperity as members of the medieval guild of butchers. Over time, however, the fragility of the economy in the Ore Mountains *(Erzgebirge)* revealed itself first among younger sons of the family who were trained in the cottage industry of stocking-weaving. By the early decades of the 19th century, that local economy too, began to unravel as industrialization, the arrival of the railroad, and finally the potato famine of the 1840s swept away the family's hold on prosperity and social standing.

But the book's purpose is not genealogical nor strictly local, neither in the German nor in the later American context. To be sure, the *boom and bust* cycle of Colorado's history since the mid-19th century emerges in the story of the Roeber family as well as other families with whom they intermarried. In one sense, then, the western Colorado story appears in some respects to be a version of a similar tale of social, economic, and political pressures which German-speakers brought with them when some chose to emigrate from their places of origin where they had lived for generations. Historians of immigration all agree that, from the earliest days of European arrival in North America, economic and social stresses at home explain why those who were able to do so made the decision to leave. We also know that the major story of migration took place within Europe, that is, many people remained in Europe and opted for improved conditions that did not involve crossing oceans. However, the very poorest of Europe's poor never enjoyed any such option.

Geographically speaking, the Roeber family represented the mid-nineteenth century pattern of emigration from central and eastern areas of the North German Confederation, unlike the migrations of the American colonial era whose German-speakers came predominantly from the German Southwest and the Swiss Confederation.

The migration of Europeans across the North American continent usually produced settlements where arrivals sought out others who spoke their language, followed their "food ways" and could be identified as Protestant, Roman Catholic, Jewish, or Eastern and Oriental Christian Orthodox in religion. But here too, many could not count on pastoral presence or support, and they often ended up worshipping with whatever version of church or synagogue happened to be accessible given the limitations of travel and the challenges posed by weather. Also, true to larger cultural and societal patterns, it was the wives and mothers who were more often the faithful than their husbands and sons.

Regarding the structure of families, divorce occurred in the North American West in ways that would not have been possible in Europe. As early as 1824, Indiana's courts were inclined to grant divorce not just on the grounds of adultery, abandonment and cruelty but for any grounds the courts were willing to hear. That fact made Bertha's divorce from her second husband relatively easy. But one cannot help but wonder if her daughter-in-law's untimely death in 1901 did not play a role in de-stabilizing the twentieth-century marriages of Theodore and Maria's children. Mary, the eldest daughter, would divorce; as would Gus and Maggie and Gusty; Otto never married; and Louis had opted for a common law marriage before his death in World War I.

As was true for millions of Americans, German speakers endured the horrors of the American Civil War, in the main supporting the Union or the Confederacy depending on where they found themselves as the War erupted.

And, as was true for many hundreds of thousands, for Theodore Roeber that War, the effects on his health, and the social, political, and economic connections he forged in his brief service turned out to be life changing. But the long history of the family in Europe suggests that military service had never been an objective, and conscription appears to be the only reason Christian, and much later his grandson Louis, saw military service. Nor did the family, as was also true in general of European arrivals, give much thought to how their coming, or wars and displacements, impacted the First Peoples of North America, in this instance, the Ute Nation.

Those of Theodore's relatives who remained in Germany were to be swept up in increasingly bitter socio-economic and political conflicts between the wealthy, aristocratic and monarchical few, and masses of increasingly discontented middling and poor folk. This latter disillusioned group would find the critiques of German life offered, first by Social Democrats and later by Communist Party leaders, to be convincing arguments for improvement in economic and social standing. Never especially devoted to the ruling dynasty of Saxony, nor to military service (besides Theodore's time in the Grand Army of the Republic and his interest in Republican Party politics) those who found a hard, but reasonably stable life in western Colorado would have found the decisions of their relatives difficult to understand and impossible to support. Ironically, despite Theodore's role in local and county politics and development projects, the anti-German hysteria of 1917–18 left his children more marginalized and uninvolved in local, state, and national economic and political events until his grandson's generation in the latter 20th century. If one theme ties the fifth generation's concerns to those of their great-great grandfather, it is the role that water—its origins, its control, and its use—has always played and will continue to play in shaping the reputations and prosperity of all who remain committed to a life in Western Colorado.

Sources

On American divorce law, see Van Holan, "Indiana: Birthplace of Migratory Divorce," Indiana Law Journal 26:4 (1951) 515-27 at https://www.repository.law.indiana.edu/ilj/vol26/iss4/3; for European and earlier

American details, A.G. Roeber, *Hopes for Better Spouses: Protestant Marriage and Church Renewal in Early Modern Europe, India, and North America* (Grand Rapids, MI and Cambridge, UK, 2013), 269-77.

Acknowledgments

As is always the case for any historian, I am indebted to a long list of colleagues, family, and friends who have helped locate sources, corrected errors, made valuable suggestions as to its "target audience," and urged-on the completion of this book.

During the 1980s, my attempts to find evidence about the remote and most recent history of the Roeber family in what was then the German Democratic Republic were frustrated at first by the refusal of the then-Communist regime to allow anyone not allied with its politics access to any records. Fortunately, after securing contact with the then-Kantor of Saint Martin's Evangelical Lutheran Church in Zschopau, Hermann von Strauch, I was able to visit the town where this family had lived for several centuries. In the course of time, von Strauch worked with church and town records to reconstruct the names, occupations, marriages, careers, and eventual pre-Civil War emigration of my ancestors, Christian Gottlob Roeber and his wife Bertha, née Ulrich.

Both Pastor Klaus Roeber of Berlin and Mr. Michael Rudel of Gersdorf provided additional help in my attempt to establish the remote history of my family and the conditions that contributed to the decision of Christian Roeber to emigrate to the United States. My colleague, Emeritus Professor of History at the University of Hamburg, Claudia Schnurmann, provided an important review and correction of the sources and conclusions drawn from German-language documents.

These early forays into East Germany were aided immensely when Martin Mak, himself a descendant of Bertha Ulrich, contacted first my relatives in Colorado and subsequently, myself. Together, we managed to identify the sources and details of the predominantly Saxon settlement in northwestern Indiana and also document the family's later move to the German-speaking community in and around Hanover, Kansas. County and local officials in Indiana, Kansas, and Colorado have been equally generous in responding to requests for documents.

Ultimately, Christian and Bertha's son Theodore and his wife Maria relocated to Colorado. My late sister Denise (Roeber) Kossler discovered a sadly neglected but still legible series of letters in German to and from Theodore and Maria and their friends and relatives in Indiana and Kansas. I transcribed these letters and have used them in what follows. Both of my brothers, Mark and Chad Roeber have also helped to locate and identify remaining sources in Colorado, and they also re-traced by car the probable routes the family followed in reaching the Western Slope. I have identified, wherever needed, my own interviews with relatives and neighbors that once again required revision and re-statement of what oral histories and memories claimed to have been true.

The book's most challenging chapter comes at the end. Once an author begins to write on events and times he or she remembers, the task of scrutinizing one's own memory, perspective, and the tricks that time plays on us all, becomes especially acute. Nonetheless, colleagues and family members who have read the first chapters all insisted that I write a final chapter that includes my own participation in events.

Former academic colleagues Emeritus Professor John Larson of Purdue University; Dr. Claiborne Skinner now of Santa Fe, New Mexico; and my former colleague at Penn State, now Professor of History at the University of California-Davis, Ari Kelman have provided especially useful suggestions that have shaped the final version of the story the book tries to tell. Donald Benjamin has been a keen-eyed and skilled editor, and I have benefited immensely from his suggestions and observations. Donna Marie Benjamin's talented eye provided the interior design and final version of the book cover for which I am deeply grateful.

Remembering Reputation and Prosperity

During my last year as a graduate student at Brown University, events occurred which influenced my approach to this book. My fellow doctoral student and now Emeritus Professor Walt Conser, a Californian by birth, and I gained permission to co-teach an elective course on the history of the Trans-Mississippi West, an unusual offering at that time for Ivy League universities. John Larson, after reading a first attempt at this project urged that I consider what Wallace Stegner did in his *Angle of Repose* as a possible writing strategy. I considered Larson's advice but, in the end, I have refrained from disguising names or fictionalizing what I could reconstruct from surviving evidence.

As graduate students, both Larson and I profited immensely from the perspectives on the American West provided by the late Professor Jack Thomas who first introduced us to the masterful work of Bernard DeVoto's *1846: Year of Decision*. That book focuses on the confluence of crises that would lead to the American Civil War in which Christian and Bertha's son Theodore would participate. And, in retrospect, that fateful year also appears to have served as the beginning of Christian Roeber's pondering whether to attempt personal and familial survival in the New World.

Neither Christian nor his spouse lived long enough to see their descendants settle on German Mesa in Delta County, Colorado. And yet, after five generations, their descendants still remain there, even as the family has now vanished entirely from their ancestral towns and cities in Germany. Therefore, one surmises that they would have been pleased.

About the Author

The Rev. Dr. A.G. Roeber, Emeritus Professor of Early Modern History and Religious Studies, Penn State University, is currently Professor of Church History, St. Vladimir's Orthodox Theological Seminary. Born in Paonia, Colorado, he began his graduate work at the University of Denver and completed his Ph.D. at Brown University. He has taught at various universities in North America and in Germany. His *Palatines, Liberty, and Property* was the 1993 co-winner of the American Historical Association's John H. Dunning Prize for the best book on any aspect of American history in a two-year period. He is a past president of the Orthodox Theological Society in America and most recently co-author of *Changing Churches* (2012); co-editor, *Oxford Handbook of Early Modern Theology* (2016); author, *Mixed Marriages: An Orthodox History* (2018); editor, *Human v. Religious Rights?* (2020); and author, *Orthodox Christians and the Rights Revolution* (2024).

www.ingramcontent.com/pod-product-compliance
Lightning Source LLC
Chambersburg PA
CBHW051058160426
43193CB00010B/1228